"Having known Carole Gift Page for many years, I can say in truth that she is passionate about her message to women, and she is joyous herself. You will experience her enthusiasm for life as you read this challenging new book."

FLORENCE LITTAUER, AUTHOR OF *PERSONALITY PLUS*
AND *SILVER BOXES*

"Carole Gift Page's moving, personal testimony will inspire you. She shares with humor and painful honesty her own struggles with shyness and heartbreaking rejection and how the Lord helped her overcome her fears, find healing, and discover a passion for God. If you long to become the woman God desires you to be, the depth of insight and wisdom found in this book will help you discover your own spiritual passions and to know and love the Lord more intimately."

SHEILA CRAGG, AUTHOR OF SEVERAL DEVOTIONAL BIBLE STUDIES
AND THE ONE-YEAR SCRIPTURE PRAYER JOURNAL,
NEAR TO THE HEART OF GOD

"Over the twenty years that I have known Carole Gift Page, her writing and teaching have had an important impact on my life. In *Becoming a Woman of Passion,* Carole writes from a wealth of personal experience as she honestly and openly invites readers to grow deeper in their love for God."

ROBIN JONES GUNN, BEST-SELLING AUTHOR
OF THE GLENBROOKE SERIES

Becoming a Woman of Passion

Discover the Joyous Woman
God Created You to Be

Carole Gift Page

Fleming H. Revell
A Division of Baker Book House Co
Grand Rapids, Michigan 49516

Published by Fleming H. Revell
a division of Baker Book House Company
P.O. Box 6287, Grand Rapids, MI 49516-6287

Printed in the United States of America

Library of Congress Cataloging-in-Publication Data

Page, Carole Gift.
    Becoming a woman of passion : discover the joyous woman
God created you to be / Carole Gift Page.
        p.   cm.
    Includes bibliographical references.
    ISBN 0-8007-5762-9 (pbk.)
    1. Christian women—Religious life. 2. Christian women—Conduct of life. 3. Emotions—Religious aspects—Christianity. I. Title.
BV4844.P32 2001
248.8'43—dc21   2001019421

For current information about all releases from Baker Book House, visit our web site:
                    http://www.bakerbooks.com

To the women of passion in my family,
with my love—
my mother, Millie Gift
my sister, Susan Gift Porter
my daughters, Kimberle Bunch and Heather Page
my daughter-in-law, Lisa Page
my sisters-in-law, June Gift and Annette Barrie

Contents

Introduction

What Is Passion?
When Did We Lose It?
And How Can We
Get It Back?

 She was a scrawny stick of a child, thin as a windlestraw, with pale green eyes and enormous buck teeth that overwhelmed a small, uncertain mouth. At first glance, she was all teeth, a forlorn waif who looked mildly retarded because her lips couldn't close over those huge protruding teeth. She was a bed wetter, a nervous, anxious child who woke ashamed each morning because she had failed to stay dry again and was forced to soak in the tub to remove the stench of urine.

She lived in a two-bedroom tract house, too small for a family of five, in a sparse neighborhood tucked beside a woods, a world away from the upper-scale homes of her classmates. She shared a cubby hole of a room with her brother that was divided by a chalk line drawn on the hardwood floor to define her space and his. The only way to be alone was to burrow into the unexplored cave of her imagination where there were no walls, no boundaries, no fences—a place as boundless and full of possibilities as the starry heavens she glimpsed out her window each night.

She was a plain, ungainly child in a family of handsome faces. Her parents could have been movie stars, her mother a glamorous Susan Hayward with her flawless features and flowing black tresses, her father a charming Dick Powell with his raven curls and sultry eyes. She, their artless daughter, admired and adored them and yearned for a modicum of their grace and charm.

She realized early that she was two people in one. She was the shy, tongue-tied youngster who sat paralyzed when called on to speak in class and who shrank into herself when her peers taunted her and called her Bugs Bunny. This version of herself was a forlorn flower under a scorching sun, a wistful wisp of wallflower brooding on the bleak borders of a solitary childhood. Fear drove her, chained her, kept her from reaching out lest she be ridiculed, rejected. When she wasn't teased, she was ignored. She was always the last to be picked, the first to be excluded, the one nobody wanted to play with.

But in her own little neighborhood of deep woods and golden fields, of cattail swamps and rocky dirt roads trailing off to unimaginable lands, she blossomed into another person—the ardent, invincible child who thrived in her mind and heart like a fertile, indestructible plant. This child was brimming with stories of stalwart heroes and winsome heroines and adventures that overflowed the boundaries of her prosaic life. With one or two friends, she poured out these fanciful tales and became the hero, the creator and director of her own spontaneous plays.

This child feasted on limitless possibilities. She could be anyone, do anything, go anywhere. She could speak the words and become a princess, a pirate, a cowboy, a spy. She was one of a kind with a calling she couldn't define. But even at a young age, she knew her life had been marked with a purpose. Someday she would summon the courage and discover the unique pathway she had been created to pursue. This shy, graceless child with the enormous teeth and the dreams to match would someday become . . . a woman of passion.

My friend, if she can do it, so can you.

I realize the idea of becoming a woman of passion may strike you as uproariously funny, hopelessly absurd, or depressingly off the mark. "Is she kidding?" you may ask. "Passion? What passion? She doesn't know the first thing about my life!"

Maybe I do. Maybe I've been there too. You see, I am that shy, awkward child with the enormous teeth and the dreams to match. Certainly an unlikely candidate to become a woman of passion.

What about you?

How would you define yourself?

What childhood hurts or emotional baggage do you carry?

How would you describe your life today?

Do these descriptions ring any bells?

- Everything in your life feels like a chore or obligation.
- You exist in a rut of exhausting duties and demands.
- You struggle with feelings of inadequacy, boredom, and guilt.
- Life has lost its zest, its zing, its spark of beauty and wonder.
- You can't remember the last time you felt genuine pleasure and excitement.
- You want to be creative and productive, but you're just spinning your wheels.

11

- You'd give your family more loving attention if you weren't so stressed out.
- You don't feel emotionally connected with the important people in your life.
- Your spiritual life is humdrum, monotonous, or nonexistent.

We've all been there at one time or another, haven't we? We want to see the world through rose-colored glasses, but life keeps painting a vastly different picture for us. Swirls of darkness, clouds of gray, deep gashes of gloom, jagged slashes of melancholy. Somehow, somewhere along the line, we've lost sight of the original picture, the Master's exquisite painting. And in the process, we've relinquished something crucial—our passion for life, for our loved ones, maybe even for God Himself.

What do I mean by passion?

Not the stuff of romance novels, although romantic passion is certainly a vital ingredient of a healthy marriage.

My definition of passion is broader. Passion is that ardor, zeal, fervor, and surge of emotion that infuses our lives, even our most ordinary days, with vitality, zest, excitement, and exhilaration. The essence of passion is strong affection, a sense of abandon. When we feel passionate about something or someone, we feel most alive, most in tune with our senses, most in harmony with ourselves and our world. When we feel a passion for God, we begin fulfilling His command to love Him with all our heart, soul, mind, and strength.

Godly passion is a rare commodity these days. So is a thriving passion for life, our families, and our work. In our hurried, hectic, computerized society, many of us have lost touch with our feelings. We act and react out of a sense of duty, obligation, habit, or guilt, rather than from a sense of inner passion, ardor, and eagerness. Because of the unrelenting demands made on our time and energies, we are numb, burned-out, jaded, exhausted.

A pollster asked a woman on the street, "What do you think of the high levels of ignorance and apathy in society today?"

The woman snapped, "I don't know, and I don't care!"

We smile, conceding that could be our response as well. Our lives are too orchestrated, our schedules too packed with obligations that have little to do with passion. Ah, if only we could summon from our weary hearts a delicious, sweet ardor for our lives, our loved ones, our Father God.

If that is how you feel today, then I am writing this book for you. But not just for you. For myself as well. I write, not from some lofty, isolated tower, nor as one who has discovered all the answers, but as a fellow seeker who chokes on the same dust, duties, and demands you face but who thirsts for a passion to imbue the road ahead with a touch of wonder. I desire to travel on this journey with you in search of that hidden, impassioned, creative part of ourselves we haven't explored in a very long time.

Think of us as sojourners, nomads, survivors on a madly tilting planet. We stand perched at the beginning of the twenty-first century, suspended between dissonant eras, caught in the crossfire of conflicting creeds, teetering on that small wedge of time between past and future. And in our confusion, we pray we won't plunge over the abyss into the unknown, the unthinkable. We hold on for dear life as our mercurial merry-go-round spins faster and our reeling world blurs in a pastel frenzy. Work, marriage, family, career. Once we had hoped to grasp the gold ring; now we pray only that we won't lose our tenuous balance and fall off.

Think about it. How often do we pause and take a good look at ourselves, our families, our God? How long has it been since we gazed deep into someone's eyes and savored the love we share? How long since we've truly listened with our hearts as well as our ears? Are we doomed, like Emily in the play *Our Town,* to overlook the significance of our days until it is too late to taste the wonder?

I don't want to miss the miracle in the mundane and commonplace, the trivial hours stitched together in the patchwork of time. I want to look my children in the eye and see their souls; I want to hear them out before I speak my mind. I want to trace my husband's face in my memory before age paints its own somber portrait. I want to taste and feel and smell and hear and see every ticking moment before it slips away. I want to feel the passion.

I believe you want these things too.

But we rarely manage them, do we? We have so little time. So little energy. So many distractions. So many hands plucking away little pieces of our lives. So many voices spilling a cacophony of sounds and shrieks, demands and laments.

But sometimes we do capture a glimpse or a sound, a feeling or a memory, fragile as a firefly in a bottle. And suddenly that fleeting, evanescent moment takes on eternal proportions. And it is ours to savor and enjoy.

For me, the best times come when I open my heart and senses to God, when I let Him reach down into that secret place of my soul where no one else has trod, when I experience His sweet comfort, His whispering love. When I am most in touch with Christ, I am most in tune with the rest of my world.

Before we begin our journey, I must make a confession. Outwardly, I am not a woman of passion. I am too quiet, too cautious, too conservative, too eager to please, too afraid to make waves. I am often too intimidated to release myself to the blissful abandon of being truly myself without worrying about how I appear to others. I envy my younger sister Susan, a singer and ventriloquist, who performs before thousands without ever appearing self-conscious, who gives herself freely to the moment, to the audience, to life.

I too often stand outside myself looking on, watching from a distance, judging, being self-critical. I rarely surrender myself wholly to the moment, losing myself in it. My inner parent, or my inner child, or both, are still on the sidelines watching everything I do.

But because of Jesus, because He is there watching too, when my inner parent criticizes me, or my inner child feels the pain of some childhood wound, I experience the balm and comfort of His presence. Jesus rocks in His arms the wounded child inside me. Only in the presence of Christ Himself am I able to experience the pure, heady, satisfying sensation of losing myself in someone else, surrendering myself to the moment without self-consciousness. Only with Christ can I be totally myself, free, uninhibited, without pretense or facade. Only with Him do I feel total acceptance, unconditional love.

But God is teaching me to take the love He pours out on me and share it with others, with my family, my friends, my neighbors, those I teach and speak to. I am a slow learner. I am still the quiet introvert at heart. The wounded child still lives in me and exerts her broken spirit at times, causing me to clam up when I would like to speak out, to hold back when I would like to step forward, to guard my responses when I would like to be effusive. But always Christ is there too, urging me onward, reminding me of all the other wounded spirits out there who need a whisper of love, a word of encouragement, a reminder that someone cares.

Slowly, with patient tenderness, God is enabling me to become a woman of passion, a woman who is creative and productive, who can savor and take joy in the moment, who can meet the needs of others out of an overflow of His love.

Our heavenly Father desires to do the same for you. He wants to bring comfort, healing, and joy to your secret, tender, wounded, unexpressed heart. He wants you to

15

discover or rediscover your passion for life, your loved ones, and the Lover of your soul.

So come with me.

I invite you to join me on a journey of discovery into your heart of hearts, into the hearts of your loved ones, and into the heart of God, so that we may truly come to love the Lord, our God, with all our heart, mind, soul, and strength, and that we may love one another as ourselves.

Let's begin by memorizing the great commandment, the Scripture passage that serves as a foundation and cornerstone for our entire exploration into a woman's passions. I challenge you to repeat these verses every morning before you tackle your day. Emblazon them on your heart, bury them deep in your subconscious, make them part of the fabric of your conscious mind, and whisper them on your pillow every night . . . and you will begin to experience God's passion.

> *"And you shall love the Lord your God with all your heart, with all your soul, with all your mind, and with all your strength." This is the first commandment. And the second, like it, is this: "You shall love your neighbor as yourself." There is no other commandment greater than these.*
>
> MARK 12:30–31

What is this, dear friend, if not PASSION!

A GLIMPSE AHEAD: WHERE WILL OUR JOURNEY TAKE US?

A Woman of Passion Knows and Expresses Her Deepest Nature

In part 1, "Discover and Share Your Deepest Passions," we will look at the many commitments and obligations in our lives that have depleted our passion and left us overworked, stressed out, and exhausted. We will consider ways of getting off the treadmill long enough to discover what stirs our passions and makes us feel most in touch with God, ourselves, and others. We will examine the many hats—and masks—we wear and explore ways of becoming more authentic and transparent, so that we can increase our feelings of intimacy with our loved ones.

We will discover our real passions, often hidden under a mountain of duties and other people's demands and expectations, and we will explore ways of channeling our creative urges and passions into activities and a lifestyle that gives God pleasure. We will change our attitudes about our own weaknesses and the negative forces that dismay and derail us. We will see how, when we yield to our loving heavenly Father, He can transform our weaknesses into His strengths and the negatives in our lives into His positives.

A Woman of Passion Nurtures Loving Intimacy with Those in Her Circle of Love

In part 2, "Keep Passion Alive on the Home Front," we will consider ways of loving others out of an overflow of God's love and of nurturing tender intimacy with those in our circle of love. We will learn to respond to others with our heart, not just our head. We will practice speaking the truth in love and find a new level of closeness by consciously immersing ourselves in one another's world. And we will examine ways to love those who don't love us back.

A Woman of Passion Is Passionate about Her Savior

In part 3, "Unleash Your Passion for Christ," we will recognize that it's not enough just to read the Book; we must know the Author personally! We will consider guidelines to help us develop an intimate, moment-by-moment walk and talk with Christ, and we will examine twelve steps to turn our devotional life into intimate, heart-stirring encounters with the Lover of our souls.

PART ONE

Discover
and Share Your
Deepest Passions

A WOMAN OF PASSION KNOWS
AND EXPRESSES HER DEEPEST NATURE

1

WHERE DID ALL
THE PASSION GO?

 It's just the two of us. You and me. So we can talk heart to heart. We can say some of the things we've never even put into words, things we've felt under the surface of our consciousness, feelings that are perhaps too vague and elusive to pinpoint or articulate. I'm guessing you have felt or are feeling the same way I've felt so many times, the way I still feel when life seems too overwhelming, demanding, out of control.

I want a way out.

Answers.

Help.

Someone to share the pain and frustration.

Someone to lighten the load and make the way clear.

We are beginning a journey of the spirit. Whatever I say to you, I say first of all to myself. Whatever advice I give, I myself need to heed it most of all. Whatever light

God has revealed to me, I confess I too often fail to walk in that light.

I do not offer myself as an example for you to follow. Our only example is Christ. Like you, I struggle daily to attain to the light God has already unveiled. Like Paul, what I want to do, I don't do, and what I don't want to do, I do . . . all too often.

But I don't browbeat myself for it. I simply try to scoot back under the umbrella of God's love and fellowship as soon as He makes me aware of my foolish wandering.

I'm going to share some things with you I've never shared with anyone else, things I've never before put on paper. It's not easy making myself vulnerable, exposing my own hurts and neediness. I'm a private person, not one to wear my heart on my sleeve. When life gets too rough, I turn inward rather than striking out. Maybe that's why I love writing novels; I can bury my own yearnings in the lives of my imaginary characters.

But not this time. This time it's me. Just me. Sharing with you. As openly and honestly as I know how to be. And I'm convinced that together we'll discover some important truths God has just for us.

First, let's get acquainted. Let's see who we are at this particular moment in time. What does your life look like? Let's take a snapshot. Does the following describe you?

You're in Your Twenties . . .

You're a high school graduate, with perhaps a few years of college to your credit. You're single, working toward the career of your choice, and enjoying your newfound freedom. You have a good circle of friends and a place of your own, nothing fancy, but it's yours as long as you pay the rent. While you're in no hurry to jump into the sea of matrimony, you can't help keeping an eye out for Mr. Right.

You wonder what the future holds and how you fit in to a world that, like Noah's Ark, seems mainly comprised of couples.

Or maybe you've already found Mr. Right. You've been married a couple of years and have a part-time or full-time job that keeps you hopping. You have a baby at home, maybe a toddler too, in a house or apartment that's too small for your growing family. Your husband works long hours establishing his career, and the two of you juggle your schedules like circus acrobats—shopping, paying bills, making sure the kids get to child care. The tender, heart-tingly romance that once drew you and your husband together seems to be lost under an avalanche of pablum and Pampers, college loans and credit card debts, housework and job demands. Even with both of you working, money is too tight and the source of too much friction in your marriage.

You knew starting a family wouldn't be easy, but you never realized how unrelenting and mind-numbing your routine would become. You eat too much fast food, spend too little time romancing your husband, and watch too much mindless TV because you're too exhausted to do anything else. Sometimes the only way you can snatch a minute alone is to lock yourself in the bathroom. And even then your preschooler bangs on the door, demanding to know what you're doing in there, as if he fears you might disappear and never be heard from again. You feel a tad guilty about not spending more time in church. But the idea of getting to Sunday school on time with a nursing infant and a rambunctious toddler poses the greatest challenge of your week. You hope God understands why you spend so little time with Him these days. But somewhere in the back of your mind you know you're the one losing out, because, in spite of all the good things in your life, you aren't feeling the joy your relationship with God and your loved ones should bring.

You're in Your Thirties . . .

Maybe you're single and carving out a satisfying career for yourself. It's not everything you had hoped for, but it pays the bills and provides a nice outlet for your creativity. You have a suitable apartment in a decent part of town and a collection of friends, family, and colleagues you enjoy. But sometimes you wonder how someone connected to the world via telephone, cell phone, beeper, the Internet, email, and chat rooms can feel so disconnected from herself, her loved ones, and God. At times you can't help thinking, *Is this all there is? Am I missing something? Does God have something better for me? Am I experiencing His passion in my personal life and workaday world?*

Or maybe you're a single mom whose Cinderella story turned into a nightmare. Fighting burnout and exhaustion, you're juggling motherhood and work, trying to keep bread on the table, clothes on your kids' backs, and a roof over their heads. You've had to go it alone for so long you've forgotten what it's like to have someone share your burden. The idea of experiencing passion in your life seems as remote as finding a gourmet restaurant on a desert island.

Or maybe you've been married for over a decade and have three kids in grade school and a husband struggling to climb the corporate ladder. Your life is preprogrammed from the time you wake in the morning until you collapse in bed at night. Car pools, soccer games, piano lessons, dance classes, swim lessons—you name it, it's on your agenda. Your daily routine requires the scheduling stratagems of a potentate ruling a small kingdom.

You drop the kids off at school on your way to work, pick up the dry cleaning at lunchtime and make a hair appointment for yourself and dental appointments for the kids, pick up the kids after school, deliver your daughter to dance class, your older boy to soccer, the younger to his swim lesson, shop for groceries, pick up takeout, stop at the ATM for more cash, collect the kids, and greet hubby at home, where your family chows down the fast food before the evening's social, professional, or church-related commitments begin.

Even when you snag a few private moments with your husband, you find yourselves bickering over bills or tensions mounting over trivial irritations. You wonder where the tenderness went. And somewhere amid the busyness you find yourself wondering where the joy is. Your life is so harried and overextended that you've switched on the autopilot and forgotten what it means to savor the moment. It's an odd paradox. You're doing more and enjoying it less. Doing more for God and enjoying Him less too. When did He become so distant, so remote? And why, when your life is so precisely orchestrated, do you feel so out of control?

YOU'RE IN YOUR FORTIES . . .

You've been hearing the word *menopause* lately, but surely it doesn't refer to you. You're still young, with the better part of life still ahead. But sometimes when you look in the mirror in the morning, it's your mother's face you see, not your own. And your size-10 figure that was so easy to maintain in your thirties is imperceptibly slipping up a size or two. Your husband's looking older too, with those thickening jowls and strands of gray in his thinning hair. And when, to your dismay, he flashes his AARP card for those senior discounts, you want to proclaim, "Hey, I'm not that old! I was a child bride!"

You have teenagers now, so your house is never quite your own. At any time of the day or night a horde of hungry, noisy, chattering, laughing teens invades the premises and razes the kitchen like locusts, tracking up your clean floor and taking over the family room. But it's better to have them at your house than off somewhere getting

25

into trouble. Your life has settled into something of a routine, even if the pace is still hectic.

Maybe this is a second marriage and you're struggling to instill harmony and unity in a blended family. You work hard as a housewife and mother and probably maintain an outside job as well. Your husband is at the top of his career and busier than ever, and the two of you are starting to realize your retirement years aren't that far off. You're making more money, but expenses are greater than ever with teenagers to raise, college looming, or maybe even a daughter's wedding on the horizon.

At times you feel as though you're in a rut and wonder if there's more you should be doing, more you should be experiencing while you're young enough to enjoy it. You love your husband, but it's been a long time since you felt that sweet, fresh bloom of romance. You've been walking with the Lord for a long time too, serving Him in church, maybe even teaching a Sunday school class or singing in the choir. But you can't remember the last time you shed tears of impassioned love and gratitude for Christ or lay facedown and wept brokenly for the lost. Passion like that belongs to the young, you might remark. But secretly you wish you could recapture that tender, joyous passion of your youth.

You're in Your Fifties or Sixties . . .

Now that more of your life is behind you than ahead, you are realizing how short life is and how fast the years fly by. Why didn't someone tell you that before, so you could have savored the moments when your children were young? Now they're nearly all out of the nest. In college. Married. In the service. Living on their own. But there is one bright spot. The grandkids are coming, bringing another chance to get it right. And you're learning something important: You never stop worrying about your kids, even when they have families of their own. So your domestic horizons are broadening as you welcome sons- and daughters-in-law . . . and, yes, those precious grandchildren!

But even as your youngsters begin carving out independent lives, another unsettling phenomenon takes you by surprise. While you weren't looking, your parents have grown old and need someone to look after them. And you thought you could coast along and indulge your own aches and pains! As the "sandwich generation," you are caught in the middle and stretched to the limits by the relentless needs of both the young and the old. You may even be raising your grandchildren while caring for an aging parent. Such care-giving duties may overwhelm you just as you or your husband face health problems of your own. You may find yourself feeling depressed, apathetic, routinely going through the motions. Even your worship may be superficial and perfunctory. But no matter how busy, demanding, and mind-numbing your days may be, you recognize within yourself that innate need for zest and vitality in your life . . . for, yes, say it . . . passion!

YOU'RE IN YOUR SEVENTIES OR EIGHTIES . . . AND HOLDING

Growing up, you believed people this old couldn't possibly enjoy life. After all, they already had one foot in the grave. When you were young, perhaps that was so. Half a century ago, not many people were healthy and robust enough to make it into their eighties.

But times have changed. People are living longer and enjoying their twilight years more. People your age are one of the fastest growing age groups, right after that hale and hearty gang turning one hundred. Many people who thought life began at forty are realizing it can begin all over again at eighty.

27

Even if the young people haven't caught on yet to the fact that age brings its own rewards in wisdom and life experience, you know instinctively you could teach this younger generation a thing or two. Lots of things, in fact. If they'd only listen.

You've seen it all. Two world wars and countless global skirmishes. Each tumultuous decade has brought its own unique trials and challenges. In the midst of hardships and troubles, social upheaval and daunting financial pressures, you've carved out a meaningful life for yourself. You've achieved many of your dreams and quietly relinquished others that were dear to your heart.

Perhaps you've raised a family and marveled as your own children became grandparents. Maybe you've outlived the husband of your youth and are facing life alone for the first time. And now that you're well into your retirement years, you wonder what to do with the rest of your life. Are you supposed to sit back, give up, and just coast along into glory?

A resounding no.

It may be a scary world out there, but it's also an exciting and fascinating one. Without the burden of career or family demands, you have the chance to explore brand-new ways of enjoying life, being productive, and expressing your creativity.

May I share a personal example? My eighty-year-old mom, a professional artist and cancer survivor, has been a widow for two years. In that time she completely remodeled her house, made her family room into an art studio, painted dozens of paintings, continued teaching several art classes in her home each week, put on several one-woman art shows at the local junior college, bought a computer and learned how to use it, got on the Internet and made pen pals all over the world, started selling her paintings on E-bay, and—get this!—began dating. Now, when I talk to her on the phone, she tells me about her latest jaunt to this place or that, or about the great new outfit she bought, or she asks my advice about what to wear when she goes out or if I think so-and-so will call tonight. The other day I told her, "Mom, you sound more like my twenty-year-old daughter than my mother!" And, you know, I couldn't be more pleased.

Did you recognize yourself in any of these scenarios? It's possible none of them describes you. After all, you are a unique individual. There's no one else like you. No other person possesses your experiences, your personality, your way of looking at the world.

Now I suppose it's my turn. If we're going to proceed together on this quixotic, unpredictable journey to become women of passion, you need to know who your traveling companion is.

In a nutshell, I'm a fifty-something stay-at-home mom (except when I'm teaching at writers' conferences or speaking to women's groups). I'm a hopeless procrastinator who faces an ongoing struggle with her weight (Would you believe I was a scrawny kid?), laziness (Twelve years in this house and I still have boxes in my walk-in closet I haven't unpacked.), and watching too much TV (I admit I'm an inveterate people watcher. I figure, where better than the tube to find such a hodgepodge of quirky humanity milling about?).

I juggle the often daunting challenge of writing at least two books a year while being Mom to my three grown kids (two are schoolteachers, one a college student) and Grandmom to the three grandkids. A hermit at heart, I honestly wouldn't mind being locked alone in my house for a week, as long as I had my microwave popcorn, my computer, my books (including my Bible), and my TV.

Oh, and did I mention my husband, Bill? I've been married to the same dear man for thirty-four years, and he's more handsome to me today than he was when we were

29

dating (and, no, he didn't bribe me to say that). A lusty, red-blooded Italian, he's not a happy camper when I tell him I can't come up to bed because I'm writing about becoming a woman of passion. So okay, that's another aspect of my life that requires some juggling.

But there's one thing I can say with certainty.

About you. About me.

About most of the women I know.

We may not know where the flames of passion went, but we sense they're slowly being snuffed out by our overworked, stressed-out, overextended lives. After all, how much passion can you summon when you're exhausted, depressed, and just going through the motions?

But it doesn't have to be that way.

By God's grace, each of us can experience more passion in our daily routines—passion for life, for our work, for our loved ones, for God Himself.

And that's the journey we're on. In pursuit of passion.

Now let's look at some ways to get in touch with those passions that have been dulled, blunted, or buried.

 *A Time for Reflection*

1. Review the profile for women in your age category.
2. Reflect on ways in which your life is similar to the profile.
3. Reflect on how your life is different from the profile.
4. Consider how these similarities and differences will impact your pursuit of a more impassioned heart and life.

 *A Time for Action*

1. Begin a journal that will be for your eyes alone. Select a loose-leaf notebook or a blank hardbound book that you find particularly attractive, one you

will enjoy writing in and yet compact enough to
carry with you. This journal will capture the unique
and exhilarating journey of your impassioned heart.

Whenever you write in your journal, use this free-
writing, right-brain technique: Spontaneously put
down your thoughts as they come to you, without
editing or correcting yourself. Simply let the ideas
flow onto the page, with no concern about proper
grammar or punctuation. Record your thoughts and
feelings as openly and honestly as you can. Remember, this is for you alone. You may wish to write in
a diary style or you may compose your thoughts in
prayers poured out to God. Use whichever method
works best for you.

2. On the first page of your journal write down what
   you wish to accomplish during your own personal
   "passion voyage." For example, "I want to grow
   closer to my husband. . . . I want to find some
   excitement in my daily routine. . . . I want to communicate better with my children. . . . I want my
   career to blossom. . . . I want to know God better."
   You may have many goals. Write freely about each
   one. The more fully you articulate your objectives,
   the better idea you will have of your progress by
   the end of our time together.

GET IN TOUCH
WITH YOUR PASSIONS

 I hated math when I was in grade school. Numbers by themselves were boring. The only way I could tolerate adding and subtracting all those unwieldy figures was to imagine that they represented cowboys or knights or ancient warriors. In my mind I would picture them doing battle . . . 1,628 soldiers minus 820 soldiers equals 808 soldiers that survived the deadly skirmish. Now I was on to something. My imagination could run wild with all sorts of possibilities.

But my imagination really had a chance to shine when it came to words. I loved words. Every week my teacher would give the class a list of words to learn. While other students would groan and complain about having to memorize all those difficult vocabulary words, I would take my list and, on my own, write a short story using every fascinating word. Then I would make a line drawing to illustrate the story. Voilà! I had created something unique and special that hadn't existed before. This wasn't work; it was fun. Exciting. Challenging. And immensely satisfying.

Writing and drawing were my passions even before I knew what the word meant. I had no idea that someday my love for writing and drawing would lead me to get my B.S. degree in art education and later become an author of over forty books.

Now, in retrospect, I realize there is something in life that stirs that kind of passion in all of us, or at least it would if we took the time to recognize it. And nurture it.

Think about the things you do that make you feel impassioned, eager, and alive. You may have to dig deep to uncover how you really feel. You may have been on the treadmill for so long that you're numb; the only emotion you can summon is apathy. If that's the case, we need to stop and regroup.

SETTING THE STAGE TO DISCOVER YOUR PASSIONS

Look around you. Where are you right now? Sitting in your cozy kitchen at dawn or twilight with a cup of steaming coffee? On your lunch break at work, nervously reading with one eye on the clock? Or are you absently skimming a paragraph or two, then anxiously scanning the family room to see what the kids are up to? Maybe you're stealing a glance at this page as you sit seething in bumper-to-bumper freeway traffic. (If so, please put the book away until you're safely at home!)

The point is, for you to become a woman of passion, you need to take some time just for yourself. No matter how busy and demanding your schedule may be, you need to find a way to carve out a few minutes of time each day to pamper yourself. Relax in a hammock, curl up in your favorite chair, or soak in the tub and read this book at a leisurely pace.

Alone.

With no interruptions.

I know, it smacks of selfishness, egotism, self-indulgence. Some people actually think it's sinful to pamper themselves. I'm not one of them.

After over thirty years of being a wife and mother, here's what I firmly believe: Whether you're married or single, if you don't take care of yourself physically, mentally, spiritually, and emotionally—if you don't consistently nurture and nourish your inner person—you'll have nothing left to give your family, your world, or your God. You'll become a brittle, empty shell that cracks under pressure.

Sound familiar?

Maybe what you need right now is permission to take care of yourself. If so, you have my permission. If we were together, I would give you a motherly (or sisterly) hug and whisper in your ear, "I'm concerned about you. Take care of yourself."

Do those words sound foreign to you?

Maybe no one else has ever taken care of you. Maybe you don't feel worthy of being taken care of. Could it be that your entire life is consumed with taking care of other people? Or worrying about what others expect of you? Do you operate on a principle of guilt, constantly thinking, *I must do this or that or I'll feel guilty?*

The truth is, before you can seriously begin to tap into your passions, you must start taking care of yourself. You know the drill. Eat right. Get enough rest. Exercise. Avoid the stuff that's bad for you—alcohol, cigarettes, drugs, sweets (okay, maybe you can get by with an occasional sweet). You know when something's good for you and when it's bad. It's a matter of common sense . . . and often requires a healthy dose of self-discipline.

Enough said?

Exploring Your Passions

Before we can become women of passion, we also must discover what stirs our passions; what makes us feel most in touch with ourselves, with others, and with God; and what gives us that rare, wonderful sense of inner satisfaction, exuberance, and joy.

Sounds like a mouthful, doesn't it? Let's take it one baby step at a time.

Ready? Reach for your journal. Cozy up in your favorite chair. Now, think about the things that stir your passions, spark your emotions, and prompt strong sentiments within you. What gives you an adrenalin rush and causes your heart to beat faster? We're talking about emotions in a broader sense rather than simply what brings you pleasure. In other words, it's not just what you love that ignites your passions; it's also what you hate and fear.

Never thought about it that way before?

Envision the jagged emotion that shoots like a lightning bolt through the father who fears someone is about to hurt his child. Imagine the rush of anger and disgust, yes, even hatred you feel when you hear of incidents of rape, child abuse, murder.

"Wait a minute," you say. "I thought we were talking about passions, happy feelings, the good stuff."

Yes, but the feel-good stuff is only one facet of our passions. If we're going to get a realistic picture of who we really are, we need to consider all our passions—not just what we love, but what we hate and fear as well.

All right, you may be thinking that we shouldn't even discuss the emotions of fear and hatred. You know that popular old ditty about accentuating the positive and eliminating the negative. So you're wondering, *Aren't good Christians supposed to shrink from or deny their negative feelings?*

A resounding no.

Emotions simply *are!*

35

What we feel is what we feel.

Becoming authentic women means being honest about our feelings. Honest with ourselves. Honest with God. After all, our feelings and reactions are all part of the human equation.

What matters is what we *do* with those emotions. We can nurse our negative feelings until they turn us into sour lemons. Or we can surrender all our emotions to God and let Him make lemonade!

God wants to use our emotions for His purposes, but first we must tune in to our feelings, recognize them, name them, and then submit them to Him, to be used for His glory.

Now, are you ready for some questions? Answer them as fully as you can, in a leisurely, contemplative fashion. There are no right or wrong answers. It's a matter of seeing yourself more clearly than you've managed in a long time.

1. Focus on the three aspects of passion (love, hate, and fear). Then write down the three things you *love* the most, the three things you *hate* the most, and the three things you *fear* the most. Write quickly, the first thoughts that come to you. Be scrupulously honest with yourself. You'll find it is easiest to put down what you love, a little harder to determine what you hate, and hardest of all to admit what you fear. But you may experience a liberating sensation as you face your fears and name them one by one.

Need a little prompting?

When I took this quiz many years ago, I put down "God, my family, and writing" for what I loved most. What I hated most was abortion, and what I feared most was the loss of a child (that fear was shortly realized, but more about that later).

2. Write a paragraph about each of the passions you've listed, telling more about each one and what prompted you to feel this way. For example, you love quilting because

it was something you did with your grandmother when you were a little girl. You hate divorce because you came from a broken home. You fear public speaking because you froze up in high school speech class.

3. Write a sentence expressing how God can use each passion in your life for your good and His glory. For example, *love:* A penchant for cooking and entertaining involves a gift of hospitality that can bless your family and community. *Hate:* Your hatred of abortion or child abuse could lead you to work to overcome these tragedies in our society. *Fear:* God used my shyness to teach me to rely on Him completely when speaking in public. Maybe you've never thought about how God can use your passions for His glory. That's okay. Do your best for now. We'll answer this question further in a future chapter.

4. If you had an entire day to do anything *you* pleased, and time and money weren't a consideration, what would you do?

5. What do you do just for yourself because it feeds your soul and renews your spirit? Or what do you *wish* you could do if you just had the time, money, or opportunity?

6. If you could *be* anything you desired in life, regardless of time, money, and circumstances, what would it be?

7. Which do you prefer—working with your mind, working with your hands, or working with other people? Describe how the approach you prefer is evidenced in your daily life. For example, "I'm an accountant who enjoys working with my mind. . . . I'm an artist who loves working with my hands. . . . I'm a social worker who thrives on helping others."

8. Is it possible the primary work you do at home or in your career is not your preferred approach? For example, "I'm a technical writer, but I'd rather be out among people. . . . I'm a junior high school teacher, but I'd rather be in a library doing historical research. . . . I'm a legal secretary, but I'd rather be a seamstress."

37

If the work you do differs from the approach you prefer, describe the conflicting feelings you experience. Can you think of ways to utilize more fully the technique you prefer? For example, if you're a copy editor who would rather be out interacting with people, you might consider teaching a Sunday school class or leading a women's Bible study. If you're a college professor who would rather be working with your hands, take a weekend art class. Even if you can't change careers, find some way to indulge that area of your life you most enjoy.

Or perhaps you find that you truly enjoy not just one but two or three of these methods. You love painting, but you also enjoy teaching others to paint. You're a computer programmer who gets a kick out of running her own business. My passion for writing (the mind) won out over my love of drawing and painting (the hands), but over the years I've come to enjoy teaching writers and speaking to women's groups (people). And, of course, some occupations require that you possess skills in more than one area. A lawyer or a physician had better have a good mind and also be skilled at dealing with people. The same rule applies to teachers.

After answering these questions, do you have a better sense of who you are, what you like, and what's important to you? You may have only begun to scratch the surface of long-buried emotions. The sad truth is that many of us have never really gotten acquainted with our inner selves, the person we are under all the layers of personal, family, and professional commitments. We have allowed ourselves to drift from one activity to another, from one job to another, from one obligation to another without ever analyzing whether it's something that fulfills our deepest hungers and yearnings.

But all of that is about to change, for we are on a journey of discovery. We are shedding our sense of apathy and malaise and tapping into the passions and skills that make us unique. We are on our way to becoming the joyous, authentic women God created us to be.

 *A Time for Reflection*

1. Review your answers to the questions in this chapter. Do they accurately reflect the person you are today?
2. What have you learned about yourself that you didn't know before? Or have your answers only confirmed what you already knew?

 *A Time for Action*

1. Commit to spending some time in prayer every day this week, asking God to give you His wisdom and insights regarding the passions of your heart. Surrender your passions to Him for your good and His glory.
2. In your journal, write a one-page description of yourself, not a physical sketch but a portrait of the inner you, acknowledging your inner yearnings and passions, your talents and dreams. Describe what you like best about yourself and what you would like to see changed.

BECOME THE JOYOUS, AUTHENTIC WOMAN GOD CREATED YOU TO BE

 As much as you want to become a woman of passion, there may be obstacles preventing you from obtaining your goal. Some of these deterrents may be of your own design. You may be rivaling the Mad Hatter with the vast assortment of hats you wear. Or you may not realize the variety of masks you hide behind as well. We all tend to disguise our feelings, don masks, and build facades that we hope will keep people out or make them like or approve of us. We're afraid to let them see the real person inside. We may wear masks even in the presence of God.

As long as we're pretending to be someone we're not, we will never experience genuine, God-given passion in our lives. We are too busy playing a role, acting out the part we think others expect of us. Like actors on a stage, we speak the lines others feed us and hide our true identity under the garb of a character created by someone else. Until we give ourselves to our Creator and let Him mold us into someone who uniquely reflects His glory, we will never become the joyous, authentic women God desires us to be.

FINDING TIME TO DEVELOP YOUR PASSIONS

Right about now you may be raising a very valid argument. "My life is so overcommitted, I don't even have time to think about my passions, let alone act on them. My life isn't my own. From the time I get up at 6:00 A.M. until I drop into bed at midnight, every minute of my schedule is filled: getting the kids off to school, rushing to work, putting in an eight-hour day, picking up the kids, taking them to piano, ballet, or karate lessons, then hurrying home, scrambling to make dinner before my husband arrives home, cleaning the kitchen, tossing in a load of wash, helping the kids with their homework, getting them to bed, and finally collapsing into bed myself.

"When in this bulging agenda am I supposed to indulge my passions?

"And even if I do discover there's something I'm longing to do, say, paint a picture or write a song or sew my own curtains, tell me when I'm supposed to fit it into an already crammed calendar?"

Glad you asked. Not that I have any easy answers. I don't.

I've lived with a similar schedule for most of my life. It's a little easier now that my kids are grown and just my college-age daughter is at home. But even so, my days are jam-packed with book deadlines (at least two a year), lectures to prepare, conferences to plan for (and attend!), mail and email to answer, phone calls to make, not to mention the usual household demands of cooking and cleaning and making time for my family. Oh, yes, and

41

helping my aerospace engineer husband manage our three rental properties in our spare time.

When people ask what I do for a living, I tell them I'm a full-time wife and mother, a full-time writer, and a part-time speaker and teacher. So to do everything I want to do would take about two and a half lifetimes. Like the tortoise, I'm winning the race . . . at a snail's pace. I have my own business, and I'm the sole employee. Moreover, I'm my own boss. I know what it's like to have so many irons in the fire that you're burned-out.

As soon as I could afford it, I hired a cleaning lady to come in twice a month to spruce things up a bit. She's worth every penny. While I'm slaving away at my computer, someone else is slaving away over my dirty stove.

When my youngest daughter was small, I sent her to a neighbor's day care for a couple hours each morning so I could write. Heather got a chance to play with other children her age, which she loved, since her brother and sister were already high schoolers, and I cherished those quiet hours for myself. Even if the rest of my day was exhausting, at least I had those few hours to write, have my devotions, or grab a catnap.

Do you get the idea?

There are ways to juggle just about anything . . . if you're motivated enough.

Is your mind buzzing with possibilities?

Okay, we're not talking rocket science here. We're just looking for some ways you can carve out extra time for yourself. Examine your schedule and see if there's some adjustment you can make somewhere. Could you exchange baby-sitting chores with a neighbor? Could you cook double portions of spaghetti or beef stew and serve it again the night after next (if you serve the same meal two nights in a row, your family will see through your subterfuge)? Or vary it a little. Beef stew with rice one time and ready-bake biscuits the next. Okay, so I don't pretend to be a culinary whiz. Truth is, when my husband's working out of town, I've been known to have microwave popcorn and yogurt for dinner.

What else can we do? Combine chores with fun things. Iron or fold clothes while watching TV, read your favorite novel while soaking in the tub, memorize Scripture while loading the dishwasher, get your exercise while walking the dog. In fact, walk the kids at the same time and you've accomplished three things!

And have you noticed, with our marvelous, modern cordless and cell phones, we can do just about anything while we're talking. Clean, cook, sort, bake, polish, wash, fold, walk . . . the list could go on forever. However, as I tell my daughter, please don't talk on the cell phone and drive! You're an accident waiting to happen.

If you tell me you still have absolutely no time to invest in becoming a woman of passion, then I'm thinking maybe you have a problem with letting other people run your life. Are you one of those people who can never say no? Do you hear a little voice in your head saying you must always, at any cost, make everyone else around you happy? Do you feel responsible for pleasing the whole, vast, hard-to-please world?

If your answer is yes to any of these questions, then you're exactly where I was a few years ago. I felt it was my duty and obligation to please absolutely everyone I came in contact with. If I went out to lunch with a friend, I deferred to wherever she wanted to go. If someone asked me to read and edit their dear Aunt Mathilda's second cousin's neighbor's manuscript, I read it. If someone from church called and wanted me to paint posters for Vacation Bible School or work in the nursery or serve on a committee or teach a preschool class, I said yes. Wasn't that what God wanted me to do?

Maybe.

Or maybe not.

I felt obligated to fulfill everyone's agenda . . . except my own. I wanted to make people happy by being agreeable, helpful, accommodating. If they were happy, I was happy. Sort of. And in that same vein, I was nearly obsessive about never making waves, never rocking the boat, never making demands or ruffling feathers or disagreeing with or confronting people. I avoided conflict like the plague. (And I must confess, that's still my natural tendency even today. I'd much rather be miserable than feel I was making someone else miserable.)

In other words, for as long as I can remember, I've wanted everyone to like me and approve of me. Still do. Okay, I'll confess something else. I really want you to like me and approve of what I'm saying to you in this book. I really, really want to help you and make you happy. No, happy doesn't cut it. I want to see you become so spiritually and emotionally connected with God, yourself, and your family that it revolutionizes your life. So you see, that old pattern of wanting to please is still lingering inside me.

I think you may feel that way too, even if you find it difficult to admit it. Down deep, you know you want people to like you and approve of you. It's programmed into our basic human nature. Even when we try to push away the feeling and insist we're too mature and sophisticated for such nonsense, that niggling little sensation flutters inside us when we meet someone new. The thought may not even be conscious, but it's there nonetheless: *I hope they like me. I hope I'm making a good impression.*

I believe the need to please is ingrained in the female psyche. And that's not so bad. In fact, it's a wonderful virtue, if the one we want to please is God. And, of course, a godly, virtuous wife will want to please her husband and children as well.

So how can we tell whether our desire to please others is healthy or unhealthy? If you feel like a doormat, you need to pick yourself up off the floor, brush yourself off, and develop a backbone. If you feel as if you've lost yourself in other people's agendas, you need to send out a search party and bring yourself home. If you're wearing so many hats that you could go into business selling derbies, berets, panamas, and sombreros, then it's time to shed those excess hats and make some major changes.

The secret I've learned over the years is to be selective about the hats I wear. Not every hat fits. Not every hat looks good on me. Not every hat feels comfortable. But the minute I put on the right hat, I know it. It looks good, feels good, makes me hold my head higher, and puts a spring in my step.

When you're wearing the right hat, you know it. When you put on too many hats, you feel top-heavy, burdened down, exhausted. Before you know it, you take a tumble and fall flat on your face. And where does that leave all your pretty hats? Crushed on the pavement or rolling in the wind.

So how do we solve the hat problem? Stop wearing hats altogether? Of course not! We set priorities and learn to say no. Such a little word with such awesome power. No.

It has the power to free us from commitments and obligations God never asked us to bear. Let's talk about this huge little word *no*.

I've learned to say no to many good things in order to say yes to what I believe God has called me to do. God has called me to be a wife and mother. That means my family is a major priority. God has also called me to a writing-speaking-teaching ministry. So if an editor asks me to write a book on a subject I can be passionate about, I'll probably sign the contract. If I'm invited to teach at a writers' conference, I'll likely accept. And if a women's group asks me to speak at their Mother's Day luncheon or spring retreat, I'll be inclined to say yes. Because all of these opportunities are in the area of my calling.

But if someone asks me to serve on the social committee, sing in the choir, teach a children's Bible class, serve as the Sunday school secretary, or organize a women's prayer group, I'll say no with hardly a pang of conscience. After all, why should I steal a ministry opportunity from someone who is truly called to one of those areas of service?

It has taken me many years to learn when to say no. At first I felt God was calling me just to write short stories and novels with a Christian theme. Then He opened the door for me to write Sunday school curriculum materials, poetry, articles, and a variety of nonfiction books.

Early in my career, God opened a door I never would have expected—to teach creative writing at Biola University in La Mirada, California, and to speak at writers' conferences around the country. At first, because I was terrified of public speaking, I resisted those opportunities. But God—and my husband—nudged me until I knew the Lord was calling me to nurture and mentor young writers. God's grace was greater than my terror, so I began to teach.

Some years later God began nudging me to share my testimony with others. At first I thought I had no testimony. What was there about my rather prosaic life that anyone would want to hear? All right, I had prevailed against death more than once and nullified a doctor's warning that I would be nothing but a vegetable. I had overcome extreme shyness and rejection to carve out a writing-teaching ministry. And I had survived the death of my youngest child and discovered that God can bring joy and blessing out of even our greatest tragedies.

So maybe I did have something to say.

What could you be accomplishing for Christ and yourself and your family if you weren't snowed under with so many obligations that God never gave you? Is there something or someone in your life you need to start saying no to so that you'll have time for the work God has called you to do? What frivolous or unnecessary activities can you pare from your schedule to give you the freedom to obey God's voice?

BECOME
THE JOYOUS,
AUTHENTIC
WOMAN GOD
CREATED YOU
TO BE

ELIMINATING HINDRANCES ON THE PASSION JOURNEY

Okay, we've established that you *can* find time to become the woman of passion God wants you to be if you're selective about your hats. But the hats you wear may be just the "tip" of your problem, so to speak. We need to look at some other behaviors that may hinder your passion journey. We've mentioned them already.

The masks we hide behind.

And the fences we erect.

When I was growing up, I had so many fences around me, I probably looked like Fort Knox. I erected fences to keep others out and barricades to protect the hurting person I was inside.

Except for a few family members and close friends, I kept everyone else at a distance, although at the time I truly believed they chose to keep their distance from me. I was awkward and shy and homely. How I envied my gregarious younger sister, who could immediately charm the socks off the most aloof stranger, or my handsome younger brother, who was the epitome of "cool," long before the word became trite and overused.

So what do we do about the masks we wear and the fences we have built around ourselves?

We're going to keep this simple, since this isn't Psychology 101, and I'm no shrink. And, granted, you probably know most of this already. But sometimes when you hear something phrased a little differently, it strikes you as if you were hearing it for the first time. You may be at a place where you're finally ready to hear it, and it hits home.

That's how it was for me.

47

Some years ago I was taught by a man who seemed to see beyond my masks and fences to the very heart of me. Dr. Richard Dickinson was not only my Sunday school teacher, he was also a Christian psychologist. And week after week he combined scriptural truths with psychology in a way that helped me better understand myself. His teachings were both liberating and exhilarating. For the first time I understood some of the reasons for my own feelings and behavior. And through his teachings I came to have a better understanding of myself before my Father God.

One day I encouraged Dr. Dickinson to write a book that would help others as I had been helped. He liked the idea but wasn't sure about the particulars of writing a book and getting it published. As if the Lord had put the very words in my mouth, I blurted, "I'll help you write it, and I'll find a publisher."

The result of our literary alliance were the books *The Child in Each of Us* and *The Child in Each of Us Workbook.* Many of us learn important life principles by reading a book; I had the opportunity of discovering essential personal truths by helping Dr. Dickinson write his book. I realized I had spent much of my life hiding behind masks and fences to protect my vulnerable secret self (my inner child, if you will). I had taken on many identities in my desperate effort to be liked and accepted: obedient, acquiescent child; exemplary student; docile introvert; compliant friend. To the world at large I imagine I appeared quiet, studious, passive, and appeasing, while inside I was struggling with great, sweeping emotional yearnings and needs.

As a result of coauthoring Dr. Dickinson's book, I glimpsed the painful truth: I was spending much of my life wearing perfectionist masks and hiding behind protective walls to keep from exposing the real me. What I didn't understand was that until people knew the actual me, I could never experience genuine love and acceptance, for I would still be convinced that if they really knew me, they would reject me. From Dr. Dickinson I learned the importance of removing the masks, unlocking the door, and letting people see the true person inside, with all my needs, hopes, dreams, and flaws.

The amazing thing I discovered as I began to share myself with others was that they, in turn, began to share themselves with me. As I made myself more vulnerable, they felt comfortable to disclose their needs and imperfections too. The more I was able to communicate my inner self to others, the greater emotional connection I felt with them and they with me.

In other words, if we want to feel close to someone, we have to risk being ourselves and let the chips fall where they may. Not everyone will like us, but as we become authentic, transparent women, we can deepen the important relationships in our lives. And remember, as we choose to disguise or reveal ourselves, we set the standard for others either to camouflage or disclose themselves to us.

Try it sometime. When you're in a room full of strangers—whether you're waiting to take a test or see the doctor or have an interview—you'll notice everyone around you looks as solemn and uptight as you feel. Each person is in her own private sphere, stoic, stone-faced, behaving as if no one else is in the room. On a lark, try turning to your neighbor and confessing your feelings at the moment: "Boy, am I scared" (or nervous . . . or worried . . .). Chances are, your neighbor will relax, break into a smile, and admit, "Yeah, me too!"

There's something about confessing our neediness to another person that breaks down barriers. The very thing that we fear will make them think less of us is often the key to unlocking their private world. It's not easy—sometimes it takes raw courage—but the more vulnerable and transparent we become before God and our loved ones, the more we will feel genuinely loved and accepted by them.

Remember the statement in the first section of this book? A woman of passion knows and expresses her deepest nature. In chapter 2, you got acquainted with your passions. Now, as you finish this chapter, I hope you have a better idea of how to express your deepest nature by removing masks, knocking down barriers, and communicating to others the person you are in your inmost heart. But our passion journey is just getting started. In the next chapter we will discuss how to channel our passions into creative activities and lifestyles that will honor God and give Him pleasure.

 *A Time for Reflection*

1. In this chapter we touched on a number of circumstances that can hinder your efforts to become a woman of passion: time constraints, overcommitment (wearing too many hats), exhaustion, inner conflicts (wearing masks to hide your vulnerable self), and a wounded spirit (erecting barriers to keep others out). Spend some time reflecting on any issues in your life that can hinder your goal to become an authentic, joyous woman of passion.

2. Spend some time in prayer, entreating God to reveal to you truths about yourself that will assist you in becoming the woman He created you to be.

 *A Time for Action*

1. Write freely, spontaneously in your journal about how you see yourself today. Are you a joyous, transparent woman who shares herself easily with others? Do you wear so many hats that you trudge through life exhausted and resentful? Do you find yourself erecting barriers to keep others out? Or do

you hide behind carefully designed masks (false faces) to ensure that others like you?

2. The masks we wear are roles we play to hide our feelings of inadequacy and to disguise the needy, wounded, complex person inside. Listed below are some of the masks we may wear. Check any that you've worn lately. Make up names (or make drawings) of masks you've worn that aren't listed here.

_____Miss Perfect (I'm so divinely fine, I never make a mistake.)

_____Miss Happy-Go-Lucky (Nothing gets me down.)

_____Miss Poor Little Me (Please feel sorry for me.)

_____Miss Self-Reliant (I don't need anybody and that means you!)

_____Miss Good-time Girl (Hey, I'm always ready for a good time.)

_____Miss Martyr (Sacrifice is my name, subservience is my game.)

_____Miss Mother Earth (I'll mother the world if you let me.)

_____Miss Superwoman (I can do it all with one hand behind me.)

_____Miss Butterfingers (I'm so helpless; please do it for me.)

_____Miss Scaredy-Cat (I need someone strong to protect me.)

_____Miss Daredevil (Hey, buddy, I'll risk anything for fun.)

_____Miss Footloose and Fancy Free (Whee! Nothing matters to me.)

_____Miss Goody Two-Shoes (Wow, I'm so good, I can do no wrong.)

_____Miss Woe Is Me (Boo-hoo! Nothing ever goes right for me.)

_____ Miss Workaholic (The job is my life, my master, everything.)

_____ Miss Laugh a Minute (Ha! Everything's a big, fat joke.)

_____ Miss Merry Sunshine (Isn't life a big wonderful warm fuzzy!)

3. Describe how you want to change yourself and/or your circumstances in the days ahead. (For instance, "I will stop wearing so many hats. . . . I will try to be more transparent with those I love. . . . I will stop wearing masks that hide the real me. . . . I will express myself more honestly with my family. . . . I will communicate on a deeper level with God.")

4. Now be even more specific about the actions you wish to take in the days to come. (For example, "I will resign from any social committees or organizations that don't interest me or utilize my abilities. . . . I will begin a Bible study with my neighbors. . . . When I meet someone new, I will take the initiative to get acquainted rather than waiting for her to start a conversation. . . . I will lovingly express my needs to my husband rather than expecting him to guess what I'm feeling.")

5. Every day this week pray this verse from Psalm 90:17: "And let the beauty and delightfulness and favor of the Lord our God be upon us; confirm and establish the work of our hands, yes, the work of our hands, confirm and establish it" (AMPLIFIED).

4
TRANSFORM
YOUR PASSIONS INTO
GOD'S PLEASURE

 He knew there was something he was supposed to be doing, something or someone he should remember. But the borders of his mind had closed in like the walls of a dark cavern that have imploded and left only eddies of blackness and swirling dust. It was like being swallowed whole by death, the relentless converging of shadows and silence, then a deep, dazed slumber of the mind. . . .

The man I'm describing was featured some time ago on a program on public television that explored the mysterious workings of the brain. A brilliant composer, conductor, and pianist, he had suffered irreversible brain damage that caused him to have a memory span of little more than three minutes.

Can you imagine what it would be like to remember nothing that had happened to you more than three minutes ago? Your entire past, your loved ones, your career, everything that made you the person you are would be virtually erased.

That's how it was for this man. Reduced to a sad, mocking shadow of his former self, he remained in a constant state of awaking from a shadowy world of forgetfulness.

And so it was, each time his wife came to the hospital to visit him, he greeted her as if this were their first meeting in years. Bursting with enthusiasm, he would marvel that he had just awakened from an incredibly long sleep. Now, having regained consciousness, he was ready to begin his life afresh.

Each time, in his eagerness, he seized his journal and began to scribble down his feelings and impressions. But after a minute his pencil slowed and his thoughts were left dangling . . . until the next time he would rouse and again scrawl out the words, "I have just awakened after a long season of darkness."

An incredible tale, isn't it? But absolutely true.

Perhaps this story touches me so much because I nearly suffered the same fate as this man. At age three, on a muggy September day while staying at my grandparents' home in Marion, Indiana, I was bitten by a mosquito carrying sleeping sickness. (You may have seen the film *Awakenings*, which shows the grim consequences that can ravage those suffering from this disease.) I went into convulsions as my parents made the interminable drive to Children's Hospital in Indianapolis. There, I slipped into a coma and was hospitalized for the next ten days while doctors tried to determine what was wrong with me. With the diagnosis of encephalitis (an inflammation of the brain), the doctors told my parents I might not survive. They added that it would probably be best if I didn't, since I would likely be nothing but a vegetable.

My mother, a young Christian, refused to accept their prognosis. She prayed and promised God my life if He would heal me. Praise Him, He did. (As far as I know, the only residual effect is that I have absolutely no sense of direction, nor can I visualize where I've been or where I'm going, no matter how often I retrace the same ground. Don't even ask me to describe what the house across the street looks like. I can't.)

In my earliest memory, I'm standing in a crib in a large, sterile-looking room next to a square pillar. There's nothing in the crib except a sheet, not even a blanket or a toy. I'm clutching the metal bars and watching a closed door—a door that never seems to open—and screaming for my mother. (My mother tells me they wouldn't let her visit because it made me too upset, but she could hear my screams echoing down the hospital corridor.)

I grew up hearing the story of how I had narrowly escaped being a vegetable, of how I, like the woeful composer, had awakened after a long season of darkness.

But, sadly, the composer is doomed to wake over and over again out of the same endless sleep, only to slip back into the miry darkness minutes after his awakening.

This story intrigues me. I see in it a remarkable parable. Do you see it too? Many of us have something in common with this man.

We are in a constant state of beginning, of awaking out of our spiritual sleep to the possibilities of what we can become as women of God, as women surrendered heart and soul to Jesus Christ.

Maybe it was a sermon, or our own Bible reading or prayer, or a crusade, or a praise song or hymn, or a retreat speaker, or the words of someone we love that stirred that yearning within us to be all we could be for Christ, to wake out of our self-imposed slumber, to reach out and grasp that next spiritual plateau, to make real the vision of all we could accomplish for Him.

But after our initial burst of enthusiasm, we settle back and let the vision die . . . until the next time something or someone stirs that dream within us.

Why is it that we remain forever on the threshold of our potential, that we don't follow through, that we don't catch and hold the dream and turn it into reality?

In this chapter we're going to talk about turning dreams into reality. We're going to look at ways we can channel our passions into creative activities and lifestyles that will honor God and give Him pleasure.

Does that sound strange to you? Wanting to do something that gives God pleasure? Maybe it never occurred to you that the almighty God of the universe would choose to take pleasure in you. He does. That's why He made you. To have fellowship with Him. It gave Him pleasure to create us.

WE ARE IMAGE BEARERS OF A CREATIVE GOD

Open your mind to the truth of who we are. We're not accidental by-products of a serendipitous universe that blundered into existence during some cosmic pyrotechnic show. We are children of a creative God. Scripture begins with God creating. He created the heavens and the earth, the land and the sea, night and day, and all living creatures. People. Animals. Birds. Fish. Don't you suppose God had an absolutely marvelous time creating all the critters and gizmos and gadgets and doohickeys on our planet? After all, it's part of His nature to create, to breathe life into things. And because we are made in His image, a love for creativity is a vital and intrinsic part of our nature too.

All you have to do is look around you to see how incredibly joyous and jubilant God must have been when He created our world. You need only look at the vast array of crazy, colorful, cuddly—and not so cuddly—creatures He created to realize He was having a jolly good time. And

I'm sure on more than one occasion He laughed uproariously as He put the finishing touches on some of His creations—the duck-billed platypus, the giraffe, the octopus, the starfish, the orangutan.

And if you still doubt God's rollicking sense of humor, just stand on a street corner someday and watch the quirky, comical, ragtag collection of humanity that passes by. Don't tell me God wasn't smiling when He created us.

God could have gotten by with creating a smaller, rather drab universe, with maybe only a few stars and a handful of galaxies. He could have fashioned fewer animals, fewer flowers, fewer species and varieties of everything. He could have made a black-and-white world, and we wouldn't have known the difference. He could have given us infinitely fewer choices of food and habitats, climates and environs, plus limited editions of our fellow creatures. He could have made the whole world a plain in Kansas, or the Sahara Desert, or Iceland. He could have gotten bored with creating and stopped with turnips or gnats or chimpanzees. The point is, God gave creation the full benefit of His omnipotence, and He obviously took immense pleasure in what He did, for when He was finished, He looked around, smiled to Himself, and said, "Yes, it is good!"

With God as our example, you can see that we face an enormous standard of excellence. Our heavenly Father could have said, "Creativity is My domain; I don't choose to share it with you." Instead, He gave us hearts that yearn to create something beautiful for Him and something beautiful for ourselves as well. We are all creative. Yes, that means you too. The fact that creativity comes in so many hues and sounds and flavors and textures and forms is testimony to the vast and dazzling imagination of our Father God. The urge to create is as much a part of us as our longing to be loved and cherished. And, oh, how we desire for God to take pleasure in us.

I do. Don't you?

OUR PASSIONS AND GOD'S PLEASURE

Remember the inspiring true story of the 1924 Olympic champion Eric Liddell, told in the film classic *Chariots of Fire?* After winning the gold medal, he later went on to become a missionary to China and eventually died in a Japanese prison camp. But he lived a life filled with unswerving dedication and passion for God. In fact, he made a comment that many will long remember. He said, "When I run, I feel God's pleasure."

Oh, what a world of meaning in those few simple words!

Years ago, when I first heard Liddell's comment, something crucial clicked in my brain. It was one of those priceless moments we call epiphanies, when some seemingly insignificant detail strikes such a resounding chord of truth within us that it changes our life forever.

Eric Liddell's handful of words said it all. That was exactly how I felt, but I had never found the words to express it before. But, of course, for me, it wasn't running. (Believe me, neither God nor I would take any pleasure in seeing me run.) No, for me it was this: *When I write, I feel God's pleasure!* I sense that deep, inner conviction that this is what God created me to do! Even as I write these words, I am experiencing that inner sense of calling, the sensation that what I am doing this moment gives God pleasure. Why? Because it is the calling I believe He has placed on my life. Therefore, for me to do what He has called me to do is an act of worship and obedience to Him.

Worship, because as I write about Him, as I grope for mere words to articulate the vast shape and substance of His elusive truths, praise and adoration rise in my heart for my Father God.

And *obedience,* because, if He has indeed called me to write, I must obey and sit myself down at my computer . . . and write! Sometimes it's hard work. Sometimes I'd rather be doing something else. Anything else! Sometimes the right words won't come, and I feel as if I am turning myself inside out or pouring myself out to say what God prompts me to say.

Whatever God has called us to do, surprisingly, it isn't the end results that matter most to Him. It's not how many books you write or lessons you teach or songs you sing. No, it's the process. It's our continuing act of worship and obedience to Him as we fulfill the purpose to which He has called us.

And another thing. God is more interested in how the process impacts us than in how we impact the process. In other words, God isn't looking at the books I write so much as He is watching the person I become as I obey His calling moment by moment, hour by hour, day by day. Am I becoming more loving and Christlike, exemplifying the fruits of His Spirit? Am I daily being conformed to the image of His Son? Am I keeping my passion for Him alive in my heart by spending time every day in His presence? Those are the questions God cares about as we pursue the work He has given us.

So for me, my most significant privilege in writing is to experience God's pleasure. Anything else—being published, achieving fame and fortune, even helping my fellow human beings—is secondary, frosting on the cake, to my highest calling of giving God pleasure. Worldly success is of little importance in the grand scheme of things.

What do *you* do that gives God pleasure?

Maybe the question never occurred to you before.

Maybe your initial reaction is, nothing!

That's not true.

God has given every one of His children something to do that when they are obedient in pursuing it they will experience that heady, exhilarating sensation in their souls . . . God's pleasure.

When my sister, Susan, a Christian entertainer, sings, she feels God's pleasure.

59

When my mother, an accomplished artist, paints, she feels God's pleasure.

Let me ask again. What do *you* do that makes you feel God's pleasure?

Maybe you haven't discovered it yet. Ask yourself, "What makes me feel most satisfied, most obedient to God, most in tune with His Spirit? What gives me a warm, transcendent feeling? What makes me feel I'm doing what God called me to do? What was I born to accomplish?"

It could be anything—teaching a Sunday school class, doing your best at your job, starting your own company, rocking your baby, painting a picture, singing a song, witnessing, taking someone a meal, helping a friend, praying, listening to a troubled teenager, cleaning house, fixing dinner for your family, stepping out in faith to do something you never dreamed you could do . . .

God has something for every one of us to do that brings Him pleasure. We need to find out what it is and do it for His glory. There's no greater sense of fulfillment on earth.

I can almost hear you saying, "All right, I know I have a talent or two, something I'm good at, but it's not that special. How do I know it's something that will give God pleasure?"

First of all, know that God can use you—whoever you are, whatever your abilities, whatever you hold in your hands. David, the shepherd boy, had only a slingshot and some smooth stones. The boy who shared his meal with Jesus and five thousand others had only a few loaves and fishes. Many of Jesus' followers came empty-handed or laden down with burdens. They had nothing to lay at Jesus' feet except their problems, their broken lives, their fractured dreams. But God can use even the things you consider liabilities. And He can use abilities you don't even realize you have.

You may say, "I'm just an ordinary person. I can't sing or speak or witness or lead a group."

It doesn't matter. You may not see what you're holding in your hands, but God sees, and He'll use it if you willingly release it to Him.

We can gain some important insights into this matter of giving God our talents by reading chapters 35–38 of Exodus. Moses, speaking to the congregation of the children of Israel, is delivering God's detailed instructions for building the tabernacle, which is to represent God's holy presence and divine involvement with humankind. It is to be a sacred place dedicated to honoring God, and for His service.

In Exodus 35:5, God tells the people, "Take from among you an offering to the LORD. Whoever is of a willing heart, let him bring it as an offering to the LORD." Verse 10 says, "All who are skillful among you shall come and make all that the LORD has commanded." And Exodus 35:21–22 tells us, "Then everyone came whose heart was stirred, and everyone whose spirit was willing, and they brought the LORD's offering for the work of the tabernacle. . . . They came, both men and women, as many as had a willing heart."

In fact, the women played a significant role in building and furnishing the tabernacle. Verses 25 and 26 say, "All the women who were gifted artisans spun yarn with their hands, and brought what they had spun, of blue and purple and scarlet, and fine linen. And all the women whose heart stirred with wisdom spun yarn of goats' hair."

Eventually, so much work was produced that Moses had to say, "Enough!" (Exod. 36:5–6). The people's generosity had exceeded the need!

What do you notice about these verses? There's a recurring theme that illustrates God's principle for using the gifts of His children. God doesn't focus on our talents but on the attitude of our hearts. Over and over we read such phrases as, "Whoever is of a willing heart . . . everyone came whose heart was stirred, and everyone whose spirit was willing . . . as many as had a willing heart . . . all the women whose heart stirred with wisdom . . . all the men and women whose hearts were willing."

God isn't nearly as interested in the extent of your talents as He is in the willingness of your heart and spirit. He wants people whose passions have been stirred.

Now notice Exodus 38:8, a modest little verse that is almost lost amid all the hoopla about the temple and all the endless details about utensils and firepans and grates and rings and poles: "He made the laver [that is, the basin used by the temple priests for ceremonial washing] of bronze and its base [pedestal] of bronze, from the bronze mirrors of the serving women who assembled at the door of the tabernacle of meeting."

It almost slips by us, doesn't it? This verse contains a rather fascinating detail. Here it is: The bronze mirrors (plates of brass polished into looking glasses) of the serving women were used to make the temple's ceremonial washbasin (crucial to the temple, because this laver of regeneration represented the Holy Spirit, who washes us clean from sin).

What significance does this seemingly obscure verse hold? Who cares that the bronze for the basin came from a bunch of serving women?

God cares.

What do we know about these generous women? Not much. They were serving women. That could mean they were poor women who were constrained to serve others in order to survive. Being servants, they couldn't have owned much. Their bronze mirrors were probably their prized possession, perhaps the only thing of value they owned. But they gave them up willingly for the building of the temple. They gave the best they had—their cherished mirrors.

Scripture points out that these women assembled at the door of the tabernacle of meeting. We can assume they assembled there often, so they were obviously women committed to worship and service. Several versions of the Bible, including the American Standard and Revised Standard, call them "ministering women who ministered at the door of the tent of meeting." Whatever their station in life, these were godly women who were pleased to give God the best they had for His glory.

What did it cost them to surrender their bronze mirrors? The obvious answer is that they gave up the opportunity to see their own reflections, to focus on themselves, to study their appearance. Mirrors were a rarity in those days. Women seldom had a chance to view themselves—the graceful angles of their face, the color of their eyes, the sheen of their hair.

Can you think of a woman today who can get along without a mirror? Aren't we always checking our makeup, our hair, our clothes? Not to mention our looks, our wrinkles, and our size.

What do we women do when we look into a mirror? Okay, we groan a little. But what else? We primp. We make sure every hair is in place and our mascara's not running. We check ourselves out and furtively compare ourselves to the other women in the room. When we're looking in a mirror, we are preoccupied with ourselves, aren't we? It's all about us, how we look, how we appear to others, how we measure up.

So is there something symbolic in this little verse? I suggest that by giving their mirrors to be used for the tabernacle, these serving women were saying, "God, I give up my rights to myself; I give up the very thing that keeps my eyes focused on myself so that I may bring glory to Your name." It's as if, by giving up their mirrors, they were giving up an intimate and vital part of themselves for the transcendent purpose of giving God glory.

Let's recap. What lessons can we learn from these passages about God's people giving their best for the building of the tabernacle?

- God wants us to respond to His call with passionate hearts.
- He wants us to give our talents to Him with willing spirits.
- He wants us to surrender to Him what we cherish most and what is uniquely ours—our "bronze mirrors," whatever they may be.
- God will use our "bronze mirrors" to create something that will honor and glorify Him.

What are your bronze mirrors?

Maybe you honestly have no idea of your own talents and skills. Maybe no one has ever recognized them or affirmed them. Maybe you are experiencing such feelings of inadequacy that you've lost touch with the person you are inside. You've covered yourself with so many layers of who others expect you to be that you've forgotten the real woman under all the veneer.

But God hasn't forgotten the real woman inside you. He knows you. Knows your bronze mirrors. Discerns everything about you. Understands you better than you'll ever comprehend yourself.

While we're at it, let's dispel another fallacy. Many of us have a secret suspicion that if we give our talents to God, He will make us do the things we hate, as if He takes perverse pleasure in punishing us.

Come on now, admit it. When you were a young Christian, weren't you afraid to surrender yourself completely to the Lord because you were afraid He would send you to a steamy jungle in South America and expect you to sleep under mosquito netting and eat bugs? Didn't you have a sneaking feeling that if you followed God's will for you it would mean remaining single, wearing dowdy clothes, doing work you hated, giving up laughter and merriment, and moving away from all the people you loved? As if God were an old meanie who wanted to spoil your fun.

No way!

Psalm 37:4–6 tells us, "Delight yourself also in the Lord, and He will give you the desires and secret petitions of your heart. Commit your way to the Lord—roll and repose [each care of] your load on Him; trust (lean on, rely on and be confident) also in Him, and He will bring it to pass. And He will make your uprightness and right standing with God go forth as the light, and your justice and right as [the shining sun of] the noonday" (AMPLIFIED).

Does that sound like God is in the business of making our lives miserable? Just the opposite! He wants us to reflect His love and light until our lives gleam with the blinding brilliance of the noonday sun!

The message I get from this passage is this: God not only wants us to do what gives *Him* pleasure, He wants us to do what gives *us* pleasure as well. He wants us to live joyous, fulfilled lives that reflect His bountiful love and grace.

How does this work? How do we mesh our desires with God's will for us?

Like this: As we consistently find our delight in God in our routine lives, savoring and enjoying His presence and daily growing more like Him, He will give us the secret desires of our heart, because our desires will evolve out of our love for Him and will therefore increasingly reflect His will for us.

 *A* TIME FOR *R*EFLECTION

1. Reflect on the statement made early in this chapter: "We are in a constant state of beginning, of awaking out of our spiritual sleep to the possibilities of what we can become as women of God, as women surrendered heart and soul to Jesus Christ."

Is this true of you? Do you feel as if you are constantly awaking to your potential and then slipping back into spiritual slumber? If so, consider what you need to do to break that cycle and become the woman God wants you to be.

2. How does God take pleasure in you? What do you do that lets you feel God's pleasure?

3. What are your "bronze mirrors," and how could they be used to bring honor to God?

 *A Time for Action*

1. Finish this sentence: When I _____, I feel God's pleasure.

2. Commit to doing at least one thing today that you believe will give God pleasure. Write it in your journal.

3. Make a chart listing (1) your passions, (2) creative activities that will engage those passions, and (3) the lifestyle that can result as you transform your passions into God's pleasure. As an illustration, my chart would look something like this:

My Passions	Creative Activities	Lifestyle
God	Read Bible and pray	Devotions every day
Husband	Plan romantic evening	Be kind, loving, and supportive every day
Children	Listen attentively when daughter wants to talk	Be consistently and lovingly available
Writing	Write a novel	Make writing a career

My Passions	Creative Activities	Lifestyle	
Teaching writing	Teach at writers' conference	Mentor aspiring authors	TRANSFORM YOUR PASSIONS INTO GOD'S PLEASURE
Speaking to women	Speak at women's retreat	Solicit and schedule speaking engagements	

5
LET GOD TURN
YOUR WEAKNESSES
INTO HIS STRENGTHS

 My life has always been a paradox. Growing up, I was overwhelmed by feelings of inadequacy and yet bursting with unimaginable dreams. I could never measure up to my peers in charm or confidence or popularity, and yet I felt special inside, as if a unique and unknown calling had been placed upon my life. But for most of my childhood that secret sense of being special was greatly overshadowed by deep emotional wounds.

I remember when I was six, in first grade; it was the last month of school. Throughout the year the class had made birthday books for each child's birthday, coloring bright, enchanting pictures with birthday greetings that the teacher would bind into a book and present ceremoniously to the birthday girl or boy. Every child looked forward to that special day when, surrounded by all the accompanying merriment and celebration, he or she was honored with his or her own birthday book.

I yearned for a birthday book of my own, but my birthday was in July, after school had ended for the year, so I would miss out on this cherished tradition. But during that last month of school, my teacher, Mrs. Danby, aware of the dilemma, instructed the children to color pictures for my birthday book, even though my birthday was over a month away.

At first I was overjoyed to think I would have a birthday book after all. But then the unthinkable happened. My classmates moaned and groaned over having to draw pictures for me. "Why do we have to make a birthday book for her?" they complained. "It's not even her birthday."

Mrs. Danby held firm and insisted the children color pictures for my book, which they did, some of them grudgingly, with the sparest of drawings. Mrs. Danby collected the pictures and bound them in a book and presented it to me as she had to all the others. But the book no longer represented something joyous and special, to be prized and celebrated.

I was only six, but I recognized rejection. I knew what it felt like. It hurt. Worse than physical pain. Worse than the time someone chased me and I ran face-first into a stucco wall and received a strawberry-size welt on my forehead.

And in the years that followed, whenever I opened my birthday book and gazed at the scrawled, childlike drawings, I remembered not the pleasure of having my own birthday book but the moans and groans of the students who didn't want to be bothered with drawing pictures for a shy, awkward girl with Bugs Bunny teeth and a broken heart.

I'm going to share something here that just now happened. Minutes after writing these paragraphs about my birthday book, I received a phone call from my mother in Michigan. I mentioned that I was writing about my childhood. "Mom, you don't happen to remember my birthday book from first grade, do you?" I asked.

"Remember?" she exclaimed. "How could I ever forget? You came home and burst into tears. You were devastated, and so was I."

"Devastated? You too, Mother? I know I was upset because the kids didn't want to make the drawings, but . . ."

"Don't you remember, Carole?" My mother's voice rose with emotion. "The book was filled with crude drawings of faces with buck teeth!"

No, I didn't remember that. I honestly didn't remember.

Minutes ago, as I described the incident, I knew the book had been the source of great pain. But I had forgotten about the ugly, scribbled faces with gargantuan teeth. All these years I had blocked those images from my memory . . . until my mother mentioned it just now, and those buried feelings of shame and humiliation flooded back half a century later.

Why am I telling you these stories about myself?

Because I want you to feel sorry for me?

Not at all.

I don't consider these early events of my life as something to be mourned. They were part and parcel of the profusion of circumstances that formed the person I am today—a person with many weaknesses and many strengths, with deep hurts and inexpressible joys.

I believe every detail of my life was orchestrated by God. These childhood events were God's way of sculpting, polishing, and refining me into an individual He could use. (Thankfully, four years of braces during my junior high years took care of the buck teeth. For many years my orthodontist proudly took plaster molds of my teeth—before and after—to conventions around the country to show off his handiwork.)

Often, we learn more from pain than from pleasure, more from hard times than from good times. Very early, I learned the importance of kindness, of being sensitive to other people's feelings. When I was excluded by others, I had time to myself to cultivate the fertile fields of my imagination. I learned to entertain myself, to explore my own mind and heart, to develop my creativity. I pursued solitary crafts, such as writing and drawing, and became comfortable with the inner landscape of my own soul. All of this was necessary fodder for a future writer.

I believe God uses all the experiences of our lives to mold us into the distinctive people He wants us to be.

GOD SPECIALIZES IN WEAKNESSES

We've spent a lot of time together discussing our passions and talents and how God can use them. But many of us are convinced that God can use only our strengths. Maybe you think God can't use you because you have nothing to give Him—no real skills, no unusual abilities, no special aptitudes or expertise. You look at the other women in your church, your office, or your neighborhood, and you think, *Now* they *are women God could use. They're attractive, capable, talented, personable, and successful. Why would He want to use me when He has them?*

Tell me you've never had thoughts like this.

Tell me you've never doubted yourself or winced inwardly when others seemed to be advancing so far ahead of you.

All of us—every last one of us—have suffered the pangs of self-doubt and feelings of inadequacy.

We feel so dry and empty, our reserves of strength so low, our hearts so shallow, our talents so few. We feel, in a word, *weak.* We're afraid that one of these days the rest of the world is going to catch on and see how vulnerable we really are. And then where will we be?

Where?

Exactly where God wants us.

No matter how weak and ineffectual you think you are, no matter how sordid or dysfunctional your background may be, no matter how bleak your future may appear, you are precisely the person God wants to use.

How many ways can I say it? You have exactly what God wants. Let Him transform the flawed, broken, raw material of your life into something beautiful for Him.

God specializes in weaknesses. That's what He uses . . . the worn, torn, ragtag patchwork quilt of our lives. That's the beauty of it. The miracle of it all. He wants us just as we are. He wants to use whatever you're holding in your hands right this moment.

Growing up, I never imagined God would want me to get up in front of people and speak. I had spent most of my youth trying to be invisible. I figured if people didn't notice me, they wouldn't tease me, so I made myself as inconspicuous as possible. In thirteen years of schooling, from kindergarten through high school, I don't recall ever raising my hand to speak or answer a question. When I was called on, it took every ounce of courage I had to force out the words. Not because I didn't know the answer. I almost always knew the answer. But because I had been teased so mercilessly, I found speaking in front of others excruciatingly painful.

When in junior high I decided I wanted to be a writer, I felt an immense sense of relief. I had discovered an occupation whereby I could live my life in total isolation in my little attic garret, without ever having to speak to others, face them, or subject myself to their ridicule again. I was home free! I was happy as a lark! I had found my calling, and, if I chose, I wouldn't have to say another word to a living soul. I could indulge my overweening shyness till my heart was content.

So you see, there it was. My paralyzing weakness. Extreme shyness, a heart-pounding fear of public speaking—of any kind of speaking, in fact—was what I held in my hand. My greatest weakness I held in my hand, and God said, "Give it to Me, and I'll use it."

The apostle Paul knew how God uses our weaknesses. In 2 Corinthians 12:9–10, Paul said, "And He [the Lord] said to me, 'My grace is sufficient for you, for My strength is made perfect in weakness.' Therefore most gladly I will rather boast in my infirmities, that the power of Christ may rest upon me. Therefore I take pleasure in infirmities, in reproaches, in needs, in persecutions, in distresses, for Christ's sake. For when I am weak, then I am strong."

Did you notice the beautiful paradox?

Did you catch the full drift of what Paul is saying?

It's revolutionary. It's astonishing. It blows my mind.

Think of it. Paul doesn't just endure his infirmities. He takes pleasure in them. But wait a minute. He's not just talking about what ails him—his frailties and physical limitations, his aches and pains. No, he's talking about so much more.

Is he a fool, or what?

He says he takes pleasure in reproaches. Can he actually mean he enjoys being criticized, rebuked, and scolded?

He takes pleasure in needs. You mean, he enjoys being needy, impoverished, destitute? Apparently . . . if it serves the cause of Christ.

He even says he takes pleasure in *persecutions*. Come on now, Paul! Maybe a person could handle a little neediness or an occasional criticism. But being persecuted? I can't imagine welcoming persecution.

And *distresses*. Paul, you're really going a little overboard now. We all have enough worries, irritations, and afflictions in our daily lives without inviting more. Aren't you getting a little too zealous, too carried away? Not thinking about what you're saying, is that it? Or are you using hyperbole just to be dramatic?

Paul knows exactly what he's saying. He's lived it. He knows whereof he speaks. He utters those momentous words out of the raw, lacerated material of his own hard-won life. He was a murderer, a blasphemer, and a persecutor of Christians before God stopped him in his tracks on a dusty road. Would you have picked a man like Paul to help grow your new church?

Not me.

Not a chance.

But God doesn't work the way we do. He doesn't think like we think.

God delights in using the weak things of the world to confound the things that are mighty (see 1 Cor. 1:27).

He delights in using us. You and me. Amazing!

So Paul knows precisely what he is saying when he declares, "When I am weak, then I am strong," for in his weakness he sees the bright, vivid contrast of Christ's strength, like light shining in the darkness, like sound in the silence.

I memorized these verses in 2 Corinthians when I was a teenager. I nearly devoured them, because if there was one thing I knew, it was that I had lots of weaknesses. And if my weakness was what Christ needed to show His strength, then I was His eager, available child.

HIS GRACE IS SUFFICIENT

But the point isn't just that we're weak. Lots of people are weak and are never used by God. The critical issue here is what we do with our weaknesses. Do we dwell on them, use them as excuses, allow them to make us powerless, angry, or bitter? Do we nurse our weaknesses and feel sorry for ourselves?

No. Our weakness is only half of the equation. The other half is Christ. He said, "My grace is sufficient for you, for My strength is made perfect in weakness." His grace. His unmerited favor. It's enough for us. It's ours for the taking, and in turn, we give Him our weaknesses. Does that sound like a fair exchange? Okay, so it's definitely weighted in our favor. So what are we saying here?

God wants us to surrender to Him our weaknesses, and He will give us enough of His grace so that we can demonstrate His strength. Think about the ramifications. That means we're not only saved by His grace, but we abide in His grace as well. His grace empowers us in our weakness to accomplish whatever God calls us to do. By using those who are weak, God shows His strength. Thus, the honor and glory resulting from any of our achievements go where they belong—to Christ.

In the mid-1970s, when I began to have some publishing success, Dr. Lowell Saunders, a professor at Biola University, invited me to teach an upper-division course in creative writing. I was terrified at the prospect of standing in front of a class and speaking. (Okay, I had earned my B.S. degree in art education, but one semester of student teaching a junior high class had convinced me teaching wasn't for me. Besides, hadn't I spent my entire life trying not to be the center of attention?) To complicate matters further, conference directors began inviting me to speak at their writers' conferences.

I wondered how this could be.

Hadn't God and I made a pact that I would serve Him through my writing? Hadn't He agreed to let me stay in the background and keep my mouth shut . . . and just write? What I dared not share with anyone was how tormented I still was by memories of that wounded, ridiculed child of my past.

To avoid giving Dr. Saunders an answer, I told him I would pray about it.

Never agree to pray about something unless you're ready to accept God's ruling. God prompted me to accept the position. He also nudged me into accepting the conference invitations. He nudged me in large part through my husband, who told me in no uncertain terms, "Of course you can do it. Just say yes and do it!"

At first I thought, almost defiantly, *Okay, they asked for it. I'll go and speak, and when they see what a mess I make of it, they'll never invite me again, and I can go back to my writing and never utter another word, at least publicly anyway.*

There was only one problem. Everywhere I spoke, they asked for more. My students at Biola got excited about writing. One even sold a story during the course. And I discovered something I'd never known about myself. I loved teaching. I even loved public speaking, once my heart stopped thundering in my ears and my knees stopped beating like bongo drums.

During those early years of public speaking, I learned some important lessons about God . . . and myself. At first I prayed God would turn me into an extrovert and erase all my fears. But He never did that. Gradually I realized that if He made me a fearless extrovert, I would be operating out of my strength, not my weakness. And then I would be missing that remarkable 2 Corinthians principle, "When I am weak, then am I strong."

For over twenty-five years now, I have lived 2 Corinthians 12:9–10. I speak at writers' conferences and to women's groups all over the country. And always, before I speak, I wrestle a little with God, surrendering to Him that wounded inner child who is terrified of the limelight, who fears ridicule and humiliation. I throw myself on His mercy and give Him what I hold in my hands—my weakness, my neediness, my fears.

And by His grace He gives me His confidence, His love, and the power of His Holy Spirit. Each time I step up to a microphone, I feel like Peter stepping out by faith onto the water to meet Jesus on the rolling waves. And every time, Jesus clasps my hand and holds me up. He turns my weakness inside out to reveal His strength.

If ever in my life I doubted the power of God, I stopped doubting when I saw what He could do with my weakness. Only God could have taken a painfully shy little girl with buck teeth and a hurtful birthday book and put her in front of people and give her something to say. It's all Him, not me. And if that sounds simplistic or sanctimonious, I can't help it, because every time I get up to speak, I stake my life on Christ's words, "My grace is sufficient for you, for My strength is made perfect in weakness."

And may I venture to add that the principle of Christ's sufficient grace goes far beyond the realm of public speaking?

The older I get the more I realize how vital it is to live this verse in every area of my life—home, family, career, church, and community. To be honest, the older I get the more I realize how pervasive and numerous my weaknesses are, and how much I need Christ's grace and strength in every aspect of living.

In this chapter I've shared some things with you I may not have confided even to my husband and children. I've confessed some of my weaknesses because I want you to know I'm not writing this book from a position of strength . . . at least not my strength.

I'm writing these words at 2:30 A.M. I've been at this all day, but I feel compelled to keep at it until I've found the words to convince you that God wants to use you with all your weaknesses, your neediness, your emotional baggage, your impossible circumstances.

All He asks is that you give Him what you hold in your hands right now.

What weaknesses do you clutch tightly to your breast? As long as you possess them, they will remain dark cocoons of pain and defeat. But in God's hand they can be transformed into gossamer wings. And by His Spirit you will soar into blissful, uncharted realms of service for Him.

Please, right now, as you read these words, open your hands and your heart and release your weaknesses to Him. By faith receive His grace and strength. And as His strength is made perfect in your weakness, just imagine how your passions can be ignited for His glory.

 *A Time for Reflection*

1. Spend some time in prayerful reflection. Examine your heart and admit to God the weaknesses you hold in your hands. Be specific. They could be anything, such as a troubled past, deeds you regret, family issues, emotional wounds, worries or fears, a sense of failure, bitterness or anger, or physical limitations. Describe them, allowing yourself to be transparent before God. Think about how these weaknesses have impaired your life and your service for Christ.

2. While still in prayer, open your hands wide and lift them to God in a gesture of surrender. Verbally commit all that you hold in your hands to Him. Invite Him to turn your weakness into His strength and to use all that you are for His glory.

 *A Time for Action*

1. Write a page in your journal about the weaknesses you have perceived in your life and describe ways you think God could turn each one into His strength. Describe ways you can demonstrate your faith that God will transform your weakness into His strength. In other words, how can you, like Peter, step out in faith and "walk on the water" to Jesus? (For example, if you're like me, you might say, "I'm afraid of public speaking, but if I'm invited to give

my testimony or teach a children's class, I will accept, giving Christ a chance to show His power through me." Or if your problem is anger, you might say, "My hot temper is my weakness, but I will surrender it to Jesus every day in prayer." Or this: "Bitterness toward my husband is my weakness, but by prayer and faith, I will begin showing him a loving attitude.")

2. Read aloud Psalm 100. Notice how often it lists positive emotions and behaviors: joyful noise, gladness, singing, thanksgiving, thank offering, praise, thankful, bless, praise His name, lovingkindness, faithfulness. God obviously desires that we experience these feelings as a routine part of our worship. How accurately do these words describe the time you spend with God? Memorize this psalm and recite it often, entreating God to help you become more joyful, thankful, loving, and faithful.

3. Psalm 100:3 reads: "Know—perceive, recognize and understand with approval—that the Lord is God! It is He Who has made us, not we ourselves [and we are His]! We are His people and the sheep of His pasture" (AMPLIFIED). Describe how the statement "It is He Who has made us, not we ourselves [and we are His]!" illustrates the issues we've discussed in this chapter.

Let God Turn
Your Negatives
into His Positives

 My baby's life was hanging in the balance, and the doctor didn't want to give me the news over the phone. "Come into my office tomorrow and I'll give you the results of the amniocentesis," he said in his composed, well-modulated voice.

I couldn't wait until tomorrow. I had carried this baby for eight months. The past two months had been a horrendous roller-coaster ride, with twice-a-week visits to Long Beach Memorial Hospital for ultrasounds to monitor the fluid insidiously supplanting my child's brain tissue, plus the constant threat of premature labor. As if the diagnosis of hydrocephalus weren't enough, now the doctor was implying even more formidable maladies were ravaging my unborn daughter's body.

I needed to know what we were up against. "I can't wait another night," I told my obstetrician. "Please, whatever's wrong, tell me now!"

"I don't usually like to give news like this over the phone." I could hear the reluctance thick in his voice. "But since you insist . . . your baby has a chromosome condition that is incompatible with life."

Incompatible with life?

It sounded like double-talk to me. Incompatible wasn't necessarily fatal, was it?

I grasped at straws that weren't there. "Are you saying there's nothing you can do?"

My husband, listening on another phone, said gently, "Carole, I think he's trying to tell us our baby's not going to make it."

"Is that it?" I demanded. "My baby's going to die? Then say so!"

Calmly, solemnly, the doctor told us about a condition called Trisomy 18, a fatal chromosome combination from which no child survives. Once my baby was born, she would die. She might be stillborn, or she could live up to six months.

The idea was preposterous. The reality of the doctor's words eluded me. My baby was still very much alive, kicking and squirming inside me, getting hiccups, blithely swimming in her secret sea, unaware that she had just been given a death sentence. How could I reconcile my lively, little unseen angel with death? And how could the God who loved me take back His cherished gift growing inside me?

Suddenly everything I trusted was up for grabs. I needed answers, but there was nowhere to turn—except to God, who held my baby's life in His hands.

When someone tells you your baby is going to die, it's not easy to see it as a blessing in disguise. In fact, while you're slogging through the mire, all you can do is hold on to God like a drowning person and have faith that somewhere in the chaos of pain, God knows what He is doing.

I was six months pregnant when I first learned there was a problem with my baby. I went into crisis mode. Everything in my life ground to a halt—my writing, my teaching, and any normalcy in family life. My whole outlook changed; nothing in my safe, predictable world would ever be the same. I no longer had the luxury of an on-again, off-again fellowship with the Father. I was going down for the count. My survival was at stake, my baby's survival, the survival of my entire family. I wasn't sure we would make it. And if my baby died, I wasn't sure my faith would make it. I stood to lose not just my child but the intimate relationship I'd enjoyed with Christ for over thirty years. And I knew if I lost that, I would lose myself as well.

For two months I walked a perilous road, not knowing from day to day whether my baby would live to be relatively normal (whatever that meant), or be a vegetable, or die. The odds weren't good. One way or another it looked as though I was facing a lifetime of heartbreak, either grieving my child's death or caring for a severely damaged child, along with my three normal children. The only things I knew to do during those onerous days were hold on to Christ, throw myself on His mercy, and cling to Him for dear life.

Day and night He was my companion, my comforter, my consolation. I ranted at Him, bargained, begged, wept, stormed, and pleaded with Him not to let me go. Sometimes I curled up in a chair, my palm absorbing my baby's rhythmic kicks, and imagined that Jesus was rocking us both in His arms.

And amid the turmoil, the raised hopes and dashed dreams, I noticed something crucial. Although I was struggling through the worst ordeal of my life, I was actually more serene and, yes, even more joyous than I had been months before when life seemed problem-free. The incongruity of my emotional state stunned me. How could I be more at peace now than I was then?

I realized the difference lay in my walk with Christ. Before, my fellowship with Him was sporadic. I went to church two or three times a week, participated in a Bible study, and had my own devotions on a regular basis. But there wasn't the intensive, intimate, deeply emotional kinship that I felt with Christ when my life was in crisis. I discovered that in the dark night of grief we can become acquainted with the heart of God in a way we may never glimpse in the sunlight.

A more intimate walk with Christ was one of the blessings that came out of losing Misty. I knew if God could see me through that wrenching heartache, He could see me through anything. And if I could have such a close emotional connection with God during a time of grief, why couldn't I maintain that sweet intimacy with Him every day, in good times and bad?

Another blessing evolved out of a journal I began keeping from the first pregnancy complication until what would have been Misty's fifth birthday. The journal became a book to help grieving families. I've received countless letters and phone calls from women who found comfort and help in its pages. The book, *Misty,* has been released again by Spire Books (September 2000), so my beloved little Misty has a brand-new chance to help grieving parents.

And isn't that so like our heavenly Father? Taking a damaged, unfinished baby who lived for only two hours and letting her minister to hurting hearts around the world?

If God can use a dying baby to accomplish His eternal purposes, then He can use you too!

OUR NEGATIVES

Maybe you have long held the idea that you will do something for God once you eliminate the negatives in your life. "As soon as my husband gets a job, or the kids aren't driving me crazy, or the bills are paid, or my health gets better, or we move out of this cramped apartment, or I get that next promotion, or I make peace with my relatives, I'll think about serving God."

What reasons do you have for putting God on the back burner?

Like many of us, I used to think once I got rid of some of my problems, I could focus on my walk with God. When I cleared out the clutter in my life, then I could consider serving Him.

What about you? Do any of these scenarios sound familiar?

I'm a middle-aged woman with a husband in poor health, and I work part-time to make ends meet. My teenage daughter just had a baby, which she expects me to raise while she and her boyfriend are off doing drugs. My father-in-law came to live with us two months ago, and he needs extra care too. How am I supposed to make time for God when I don't even have time for myself?

I'm a college student who works full-time to pay for room, board, and tuition. My schedule is jam-packed from morning until night, with hardly any time for myself or my friends. My grades are slipping, and I'm always exhausted. If God wants to spend time with me, couldn't He make life a little easier?

I'm a young mother with two small children and a husband who works long hours. There's never enough money or time in the day to do everything that's expected of me. Keeping up with the kids is a full-time job, and my husband complains we never spend time together anymore. I fall asleep in church and doze off before I've said my prayers at night. How can God expect any more of me than this?

I'm a single mother living on welfare with two father-less children. Gangs shoot my neighborhood up every night, and I'm afraid to go out on the street. How can I worship God when I live in fear for my life and the safety of my children?

I grew up in a home everyone thought was perfect, but what they didn't know was that my stepfather was molesting me. For years I've gone from one bad relationship to another. I can't trust men. And how can I trust God after all I've been through?

I'm a successful and respected career woman with a husband climbing the corporate ladder even faster than I. But I can't get past the abortion I had when I was young. It haunts me and makes me feel guilty now for wanting children of my own. How can I make a place for God in my life when I know He'll condemn me for my past?

My husband left me for another woman, and now I'm trying to hold down a teaching position and give the kids a decent life. But all the relationships in my life are falling apart. I'm fighting with my kids, my in-laws, my colleagues, and my soon-to-be ex-husband. God has never seemed farther away. Even if I found the strength to pray, I wouldn't know what to say.

I'm single and have been financially secure for years, but life holds no excitement anymore. Everything I do seems meaningless. I'm stuck in the same old routine, going home to an empty apartment every night, and just going through the motions. I feel disconnected from everyone in my life. Maybe I'm depressed. Once I felt close to God, but now He seems like a stranger.

I'm a widow getting up there in years. I have arthritis so bad that some days I can hardly walk. At this age,

I'm thinking of coasting to the finish line. Does God still have something He wants me to do?

I'm a thirty-something wife with a husband who can't hold down a job because he drinks too much and gambles away what little we have. I'm exhausted from working two jobs, and my nerves are so on edge I can't imagine what place God would have in my life.

I'm sure most of us face one or more of the circumstances presented in these scenarios. We may think, *Oh, if I could just trade my problems for my neighbor's*. But if you scratched the surface of their lives, you might decide you'd rather keep your own problems!

GOD'S POSITIVES

Life is always going to be difficult. There will always be deaths and disappointments, illnesses and failed careers, broken hearts and broken families. If we wait until we resolve all the negative conditions in our lives, we will never find time for God. And we will miss out on the blessings He's ready to shower on us amid our troubles.

Did you get that point? God won't necessarily remove us from our negative circumstances, but He does desire to bless us in the midst of them. How do I know? Because during the darkest moment of my life, as I held my dying baby, I felt the touch of God. Death was in the room with me, but God's solace was greater.

In my journal for that night I wrote,

It is an awesome sensation, this almost physical, tangible awareness of God's presence. His arms cradling me even as I lie here. His whispering comfort in my heart, more precious than a mother's soothing words. How can I think of loss and death when I am so filled with Him this moment, when all my needs are met in His ministering Spirit, when His love surrounds and satisfies me like a warm, protective womb?[1]

What I hope you will glean from this chapter, if you remember nothing else, is this: No matter where you're coming from, no matter how difficult your life may be, no matter how threadbare your soul may feel, you have an enormous, invaluable gift in your hands to give to God. "I do?" you ask. "What is it?" (And, yes, I hear that note of skepticism in your voice.)

In your hands you hold all the negatives in your life—the problems, issues, trials, mistakes, losses, and wounds—that have brought you to this present moment in your life and made you the woman you are today.

God wants you to give them all to Him. Surrender them. Place them in His hands. All the lousy, icky, awful, bad stuff you hold in your hands right now. Give Him everything. Surrender yourself, for you are the product of all those negative events. Ask God to take the negatives in your life and turn them into His positives. Invite Him to make something beautiful of all the dross in your life. He does it all the time. He wants to do it for you. In fact, the truth is even the stuff in our hands that we think is truly marvelous and absolutely stunning still falls far short of what God wants to do for us.

Isaiah 64:6 says, "For we have all become as one who is unclean [ceremonially, as a leper], and all our righteousness—our best deeds of rightness and justice—are as filthy rags or a polluted garment. We all fade as a leaf, and our iniquities, like the wind, take us away [far from God's favor, hurrying us to destruction]" (AMPLIFIED).

Wow! Kind of puts a new light on things, doesn't it? Even our best stuff isn't much better than our worst stuff. Compared with God's glory, what we have to offer is pretty poor.

I can almost hear you protesting, "Wait a minute! I thought you said what we hold in our hands is invaluable to God, even if it is a bunch of negative stuff."

Yes, I did say that, didn't I? Another of God's paradoxes. He specializes in them, you know.

Just two verses down from Isaiah 64:6 is this marvelous, red-letter verse: "Yet, O Lord, You are our Father; we are the clay, and You our potter, and we all are the work of Your hand" (v. 8).

Get the picture? It's not what we are or what we hold in our hands; it's what we let Him make of us *in His hands.*

Wet, unformed clay on the potter's wheel looks pretty yucky and loathsome. Gray muck. I know for a fact. I got my degree in art, remember? And I've sunk my fingers into that oozy, squishy, mudlike substance. Not a pretty sight. For all appearances, it's a heap of worthless sludge.

But let a master potter sit down at the wheel and watch his gentle, expert hands turn that lumpish blob into a vase of exquisite beauty and grace. Voilà!

Dear friend, that's what God wants to do with that mountain of flaws and liabilities you hold in your hand. Give them to Him and watch what He does. Giving God the negatives in your life implies yielding yourself as well, allowing Him to start from scratch and fashion you into the woman He wants you to be.

I watched this happen in my sister's life. From the time she was hardly more than a toddler, Susan was a natural performer, singing in church, doing puppet shows, making people laugh. She could charm the fuzz off a flea.

But one huge negative dominated her life: fear. One fear in particular. She was afraid to leave home, terrified that if she were away something bad would happen to our mother. She refused to spend a night away from our parents until she was an adult. As far as I know, she never spent a night at a girlfriend's house or even at our grandparents' home, even though my brother and I spent nearly every weekend there.

Then God called her to a Christian college in another state, several hours from home. Susan had to decide whether to continue embracing her fear or hand it over to God. It was one of the hardest things she ever had to do, but she gave it to Him and drew on His strength to overcome her fears, day by day by day. After graduating four years later, she sensed God leading her to California. Obedient to God's call, she got in her Volkswagen Bug and drove alone from Michigan, crying all the way.

Today, Susan is in full-time ministry as a Christian vocalist, ventriloquist, and comedienne. And here's another of God's wonderful paradoxes: She travels all over the country performing at churches, conferences, conventions, and schools and has won thousands of children to Christ.

God wants to turn the negatives in our lives into His positives. Look at what He's done.

Doctors said I'd be a vegetable. I've written forty books.

I was too shy to utter a word. Now I teach and speak.

My sister was petrified of leaving home. Now she performs all over the country.

What made the difference? The transforming power of God.

Let Him work in you.

Maybe you're reluctant, holding back, because some of the negatives in your hands involve hurtful things you have done or are doing. Things you're not proud of. Mistakes. Wrong choices. Downright disobedience. Yes, let's say it. *Sin*. Don't feel alone. We're all guilty. Romans 3:23 says, "For all have sinned and fall short of the glory of God."

That's the bad news. The good news? "For when we were still without strength, in due time Christ died for the ungodly" (Rom. 5:6). Lest we don't quite get the message, the apostle Paul goes on to say in verses 8 and 9, "But God demonstrates His own love toward us, in that while we were still sinners, Christ died for us. Much more then, having now been justified by His blood, we shall be saved from wrath through Him."

Let these words sink into your heart and mind. Chew on them as you would a delicacy to be savored until you experience its richest and subtlest flavors. We don't have to live under a sentence of guilt. In fact, Romans 4:7 tells us, "Blessed and happy and to be envied are those whose iniquities are forgiven and whose sins are covered up and completely buried" (AMPLIFIED).

This means, in the eyes of God, you can be as pure and unblemished as a newborn baby (hence, the term *born-again*). If you've never accepted Christ as your personal Savior, then nothing in this book will truly help you. It would be like trying to resuscitate a corpse. Until the Spirit of the living God breathes new life into us, we're dead in our sins. Psychology won't help. Meditation won't help. Turning over a new leaf or reading all the recovery books on the shelf won't make a bit of difference.

Only this will help: Confess your sins. Believe that Jesus Christ died on the cross to pay the penalty for your sins and conquered death by bodily rising from the grave. Ask Christ to cleanse you and make you a new person through His Holy Spirit. When you invite Christ into your heart, His Spirit will enter your life and you will have fellowship with Him forever.

That's the gospel in a nutshell. The Good News. I trust you've already made your decision for Christ, but if you haven't, I pray you will make it now. A personal relationship with Christ is the foundation stone for everything I've shared with you in this book. It's the one "nonnegotiable" of life.

Without the freedom from guilt that we find in Christ, we can never be the women of passion we yearn to be. Guilt will bog us down, hold us back, depress us, smother us, wither us. Until we deal with the issues of sin and guilt, we can't focus on our passions. Before we surrender our talents to God, we must first surrender our sinful souls, a lifetime's accumulation of guilt, and ask Him to forgive us and make us whole. Wholeness comes only from God. Sweet redemption. Life-giving deliverance. They're ours for the asking. Anything less, and we're chasing the wind, seeking salvation in ourselves, turning inward to our own resources, as if we could by any means save ourselves.

We can't.

Many women today have gotten caught up in the talk-show mentality that suggests we should get in touch with our own spirituality and meditate to feel better about ourselves and find meaning in life. The goal of this generic spirituality is to make us happy and self-fulfilled. There's one major problem with this brand of spirituality: It leaves Christ out.

Any spiritual quest that has self as its ultimate goal will ultimately be unsatisfying, for to worship our own humanity is to worship the creature rather than the Creator. We commit the same deadly sin Satan was guilty of when he decided he himself could be a god. That same desire caused Adam and Eve's fall when they chose to eat the fruit that would supposedly make them like gods.

I urge you, keep your focus on Christ. He loves you with a vast, limitless love. He alone can turn your hurts into healing, your sorrows into joy, your loss into gain. Let Him transform the painful negatives in your life into His glorious positives.

 A TIME FOR REFLECTION

1. We all experience negative circumstances in our lives: rejection, illness, abuse, death, divorce, failure, disappointments, loss, wrong choices, dysfunctional families. Are there any negative circumstances in your life that would be different if you surrendered them to Christ and trusted Him for the outcome? Reflect on any of the negatives in your life that God has turned into His positives. (Some-

91

times this requires looking at things from God's point of view rather than our own.)

2. If there are negative circumstances you haven't committed to God, pray now that He would take them and transform them into something positive for His glory. Be specific. Name them one by one. (If you can't think of anything, ask God to reveal them to you.)

 *A Time for Action*

1. If you have never invited Christ into your life and feel led to accept Him now, pray a prayer something like this: Dear Jesus, I know You died on the cross to pay the penalty for my sins. I accept You as my personal Savior. Please come into my life and be my Lord, the Lover of my soul, and my most intimate Friend. I love You and thank You for saving me. Amen.

(If you prayed this prayer, write about the experience in your journal and then tell someone today—a family member, a friend, a neighbor, a colleague, your minister, or someone in your church. Drop me a note and let me know too, so I may rejoice with you and keep you in my prayers. Write me at Fleming H. Revell, Baker Book House Company, P.O. Box 6287, Grand Rapids, MI 49516-6287.)

2. In your journal write down three negatives in your life and how God used them, or could use them, to bring about something positive for Him. (In case your mind is blank, consider these examples from my life: Childhood teasing made me more sensitive to the feelings of others. Extreme shyness gave me the chance to demonstrate the power of God to help me as I speak and teach. Experiencing the loss of a child earned me the "right" to minister to other grieving parents.)

7

Let God Turn Your Negative Self-Talk into "Divine Dialogues" with Him

 From out of my childhood memories comes this unforgettable comic book scenario: Bugs Bunny was on his way to visit his neighbor Elmer Fudd to borrow his lawn mower. All the way there a running conversation played through Bugs's mind as he imagined how Elmer would respond to his request.

"Elmer, ol' buddy, may I borrow your lawn mower?" Bugs would ask in his most cordial voice.

Knowing Elmer, the answer would be negative, of course. Bugs could almost hear his grumpy neighbor now: "Why should I let you borrow my lawn mower, you bum?

You didn't bring back the last thing you borrowed! Why should I lend you anything? You're too careless. You'd break it in a minute. You're nothing but a cheapskate anyway. Why don't you go buy your own lawn mower?"

The closer Bugs got to Elmer's house, the angrier he grew, as Elmer's imagined retorts drumrolled in his head.

By the time Bugs knocked on his neighbor's door, he was seeing red. When an unsuspecting Elmer opened the door, Bugs blurted out hotly, "Forget it, you jerk! I don't want to borrow your stupid old lawn mower anyway!"

To this day I remember that little comic book cartoon with the huge message. Even as a youngster, I gleaned the erstwhile truth from its simple illustration. Your own wrong thinking can sabotage you, so be careful what you tell yourself.

And that's so true for all of us. How often do we find ourselves in a new or uncomfortable situation and immediately our self-talk starts undermining us? Rather than telling ourselves we'll be fine, we can handle it, we're strong, able-bodied women, we start thinking something like this: *No one's talking to me. I'm standing here like a dunce, praying someone will speak to me, and no one's coming near. That means they don't like me. I never was good in a situation like this. I always get tongue-tied. And everyone can tell I don't measure up. No wonder they don't want me here. I don't belong. I'm wearing the wrong outfit. I look stupid. That's why they're ignoring me, hoping I'll go away. Why am I surprised? People have been rejecting me since grade school. They must see something wrong with me I can't see. Next time I'll just stay home and forget the whole thing.*

Talk about heaping unnecessary stress on yourself.

Negative Self-Talk

Much of the stress we experience in life is derived from our own self-talk, that secret conversation going on in our heads right this moment. Sometimes we're not even aware of our own inner thought life, but it's playing endlessly, like a tune that we can't get out of our mind. We are constantly carrying on a present-tense conversation with ourselves in response to life's moment-by-moment experiences. In fact, we've been talking to ourselves for as long as any of us can remember.

And what we've told ourselves has played a major role in who we are today. Some of our self-talk was good and motivated us to accomplish all that we've achieved to this point in our lives. But some of our self-talk was harmful and may have kept us from attaining goals God had set for us. If you want your life to change, change what you say to yourself. Our self-talk has power to defeat us or challenge us, to raise us to great heights or plunge us into the depths of despair. Good self-talk will produce positive action.

Even Scripture confirms the importance of self-talk. Speaking of humankind, Proverbs 23:7 declares, "For as he thinks in his heart, so is he." In other words, the thoughts that occupy your mind this minute are creating, thought by thought, the person you will be tomorrow. In the same way that your body becomes what you eat, your mind becomes what you fill it with. The person you are now is in part a result of all your accumulated thoughts.

If you're not happy with who you are this moment, you can begin to change by changing what you tell yourself in that secret chamber of your mind. And the issue isn't just what you tell yourself; it's *whom* you're listening to as well. Instead of trudging around in the mire of our negative self-talk, we need to learn to listen to God's still, small voice in our souls. He majors on the positives, not the negatives.

Have you ever stopped and listened to what you're telling yourself? What does your self-talk sound like? Many of the messages we tell ourselves are what we learned as children.

The messages in your head may sound like the voice of one of your parents. If your father told you over and over that you'd never make anything of yourself, chances are that's the message that's still playing, like an old 45 rpm record stuck in a groove.

Read the following examples of negative self-talk and mark the ones you've played in your own mind.

___ I'm just like my dad (mother); I'll never amount to anything.

___ I'm stupid; I can never do anything right.

___ I'm lazy, and it's too late to change.

___ I'll never be accepted because I'm not as good as others.

___ I can't speak (or teach or sing) because I'm too afraid.

___ I'm a weak person, so I'll never be able to give up _____.

___ I don't deserve to have nice things happen to me.

___ I don't deserve to be treated with respect.

___ I'm not good at talking (or singing, making friends, making a living, building positive relationships, raising kids).

___ I need to please everybody else before myself.

___ I'm not good enough for God to love me.

___ I'll always finish last.

___ I have no right to my own opinion (or feelings, dreams, desires).

___ Why should I try when I always fail?

___ I feel guilty for all the problems in my family.

How many did you check? None? Wonderful! Then you've already learned the art of positive self-talk. More than three? Then you have some room for improvement.

You're not alone. We can all use a little help in the self-talk department.

Not only do we struggle with our self-talk, but we're a lot more likely to let the barbs and criticisms of others pierce that tender, vulnerable spot inside us than we are to remember compliments and kind words. I don't know why that is, but I know it's true. I can receive a dozen compliments regarding one of my novels or a speech I've given, but try as I might to keep those warm fuzzies tucked in my memory for a rainy day, chances are I'll forget them within a day or two. But a critical remark will emblazon itself on my heart with a permanent and painful tattoo.

If anyone knows the power of self-talk, I do. You can imagine the self-talk that went on in my head during my childhood when I was teased and taunted by my classmates. Much of that self-talk still plays in my head today, but for the most part I recognize where it's coming from and, by the grace of God, keep it under control. Actually, under *His* control.

My self-talk changed dramatically after I accepted Christ as my Savior at age twelve. My "before" thinking went like this: *I often feel lonely and sad because I'm not popular or likeable or lovable. I can never be as acceptable as everyone else. People feel sorry for me. I'm ugly, so I'll never measure up to the pretty, popular girls. I'll always feel like an outsider.*

After coming to Christ, my thinking began to change to something like this: *I am special because God loves me and cares about me. I am beautiful to Him. He has a plan for my life, something special He wants me to do, and He will help me do it. I can do all things through Christ, who strengthens me. I don't have to feel lonely or afraid because Jesus is my closest Friend, and He will be with me always.*

That doesn't mean my thinking today is completely positive and pure as the driven snow; far from it. I still struggle with my self-talk from time to time. Here's an example I'm not proud of.

Some time ago I noticed a particular author appearing on the Christian best-seller charts. I didn't recognize her name, so I figured she must be someone new. I also began to notice full-page color ads for her novels in many of the top Christian magazines. I began to feel intense pangs of jealousy. My self-talk went something like this: *How come this new author is getting the star treatment and making the best-seller lists? I've been in the publishing business for a quarter of a century and my books don't make the charts or get big magazine ads. Why can't I have that kind of success?*

Okay, I admit, those thoughts reveal a pretty wimpy, self-absorbed, sour grapes sort of person, don't they? Well, the Lord didn't waste any time putting me in my place. A few months after experiencing those pangs of jealousy over this new author's success, I was teaching fiction at a popular writers' conference in California. After class, an attractive young woman came up to me and said, almost shyly, "You don't remember me, do you?"

I had to admit I didn't. She introduced herself, and I immediately recognized the name of the author I had been envying for months. With a luminous smile of gratitude, she said, "I took your fiction writing class at this very conference three years ago, and it was your class that inspired me to write my series of novels. It's because of you that I'm a published writer today."

Oh, my word. Shame-faced, mortified, head-hanging guilt.

You can imagine the stab of remorse and chagrin I felt at that moment. The woman I had been envying was one of my "literary babies" whom I had helped birth and nurture. She was one of mine. I was the mommy. How could I be jealous of one of my own precious literary children?

She never knew what her words meant to me that day, but they were a vivid and resounding reminder of the ministry God had called me to—birthing and nourishing new writers, literally creating my own competition. That day I figuratively fell on my face before God and begged His forgiveness for my puny, shallow, miserly vision of His grand design. I rejoiced that He had chosen me to help another writer.

I wish I could say I no longer have a jealous bone in my body when it comes to the success of other writers. I wish I could say I never make comparisons or feel inadequate. The truth is, internal monologues often run in my head. *I can't, I'm not able, no one cares, I'll fail.* . . . And I have to change gears and make it an internal dialogue that reflects Christ's thoughts: *You can, I'll be with you, I've called you, I love you.* . . .

WHOM ARE YOU LISTENING TO?

Second Timothy 1:7 tells us, "For God has not given us a spirit of fear, but of power and of love and of a sound mind." Think of it! God has already given us the tools for positive self-talk. First, He makes it clear that if we're entertaining fears and anxieties, they're not from Him. No way!

But what He does give us is His power and love and a sound, disciplined mind. How does He do that? Through His Holy Spirit who indwells every believer. First Corinthians 3:16 says, "Do you not know that you are the temple of God and that the Spirit of God dwells in you?"

Wow! You can't get any better than that! If the God of the universe sees us as His temple, a holy place for His Spirit to dwell, how do we dare go around sniveling and muttering complaints, with our chin dragging on the ground?

So how do we discipline ourselves to maintain positive, God-pleasing self-talk? Where we keep our focus will influence our thought life and help determine the kind of person we become.

99

We can look outward at our circumstances. Then we will think these thoughts: *Woe is me. Life is awful. Why does everything go wrong? Why can't I ever win? No matter what I do, nothing goes right for me. Life is against me. I'm just treading water, getting nowhere. Why can't things go my way for a change? Why do I have to endure all these trials? Other people get the breaks. Why can't something good happen to me?*

We can look inward at ourselves. Then our thoughts will go something like this: *I'll never amount to anything. I can never measure up. I'll always be a failure. I'm just not as talented (or good, or smart, or capable) as other people. I can't speak or sing or lead or teach. I'm nothing, nobody. I keep messing up. I'll always fall short. I just don't have it in me to succeed. My inadequacies will always keep me down. I'm not pretty enough, or popular enough, or spiritual enough. God must shake His head when He looks at me. I don't have it in me to get ahead. I have nothing to offer God. I'm too average, too plain, too ordinary, too weak, too dumb, and too ugly to do anything great for God. Why should He want to use someone as weak and flawed as I am?*

Or we can look upward to Christ and focus on who He is and accept His love and comfort and all-sufficiency for our needs. Then our thoughts will run like this: *Lord, You are so precious to me. You are love and joy and peace. You are my security, my all in all. You are beautiful. You forgive me for my sins. You lift me up when I am down. You weep with me when I am hurting. You gave Your life for me. You love me with a vast and limitless love. You hold me in the palm of Your hand. You died so I might live. You keep me under the shadow of Your wing. You are my Father, my Shepherd, my Savior, my Comforter, my constant Companion. You give me Your strength when I am weak. You are preparing a place in heaven for me so that I may feast on Your love forever. I am of inestimable value to You. I need nothing else as long as I have You!*

Remember Peter, when he walked on the water to Jesus? As long as he kept his eyes on the Master, he stayed afloat. But as soon as he looked at the surging waves, he started to sink. If we are to survive and thrive, we must keep our eyes not on ourselves or our circumstances but on Christ.

Maybe right about now you're saying, "Well, sure, that's what I want to do—keep my eyes on Jesus and utter only positive self-talk. It sounds great in theory, but how do I put such lofty principles into practice in my daily life?"

God actually gives us the answer for positive self-talk in three succinct but powerful little verses: "Rejoice always, pray without ceasing, in everything give thanks; for this is the will of God in Christ Jesus for you" (1 Thess. 5:16–18).

You're likely familiar with these verses; maybe you've even memorized them, as I did in my youth. You see them imprinted attractively on wood plaques or printed in church bulletins or cross-stitched on homespun wall hangings. Very nice. Yes, indeed. Lovely. Charming.

Only one problem. What they tell us to do is humanly impossible.

Oops, did I say that? Yes, I did.

I mean, let's face it, who among us can rejoice all the time? Who can pray without ever stopping? Most of us find it difficult enough just to snatch a few minutes out of our busy day to pray. And here's the real kicker: You mean I'm supposed to be saying "Thank You, Lord!" in the midst of every frustrating, painful, disappointing event in my life?

"Divine Dialogues" with God

How can I remain in a constant state of rejoicing, praying, and giving thanks?

Surely God wouldn't ask us to do it if it weren't possible. Maybe, instead of all the negative stream-of-consciousness thoughts that run through our minds—the worries, doubts, and mumble-grumbles—we're supposed to maintain moment-to-moment thinking that includes Christ. We're supposed to stay "plugged in" to fellowship with Him. In other words, we need to turn our negative internal monologues into "divine dialogues" with God.

Okay, how do we do *that?* You can see we're digging ourselves in deeper by the minute.

At this point, we might wonder how intimately God wants to be involved with us. Some people have the idea that our heavenly Father created us and then went off somewhere to do His own thing, leaving us to sink or swim. At times we may feel He has deserted us. We may fear He's so displeased with us that He has no real interest in our lives. We may even feel that we're putting God out by bothering Him so often. Maybe we should pester Him only about the big things, the real life-and-death issues.

But if I'm reading the Scriptures correctly, God does not intend to be an absentee Father. He truly wants to be involved in the ordinary, everyday minutia of our lives, the moment-by-moment incidentals.

How do I know?

Jesus said in Matthew 10:30, "The very hairs of your head are all numbered" (some versions of the Bible say "counted").

Now, that's an interesting bit of trivia, isn't it?

Why would God want us to know this odd little fact?

What relevance does it have for our lives?

You wonder, *Why would anybody care how many hairs I have on my head? Especially God. Doesn't He have other things on His mind, like life and death, war and peace . . . you know, the big stuff?*

Let God
Turn Your
Negative
Self-Talk
into "Divine
Dialogues"
with Him

Think about it for a moment. How many hairs do you have on your head right now? You don't have the faintest idea, do you?

Now, in my family, my husband has considerably fewer hairs on his head than the rest of us. But still, he wouldn't have any idea how many.

And another thing. If I can dip into my limited knowledge of science (and observation), the number of hairs on our head is constantly changing. We lose an amazing number of hairs every day. (Did you ever take a look at that hairbrush of yours?) And, of course, new hairs are always growing in. Wouldn't you hate to try to keep score?

And yet God chooses to let us know that He is indeed keeping score. Why? I think it's His way of letting us know that He desires to be intimately involved with us, right down to knowing the number of hairs on our head, which changes moment by moment. You can't get more personal and intimate than that. If God counts the hairs on our head, what other things does He keep track of?

The list is endless!

It shocks me to realize how much God cares about the smallest details of my life. It makes me want to bow down before Him in abject silence. It makes me want to worship and praise Him and beg His forgiveness for letting the connection between us grow cold so often.

What does it mean to you to know that God wants to share *everything* with you? Awesome, isn't it? Mind-boggling.

And now, in case you haven't noticed, we've come full circle. We're back to Scripture's enjoinder to rejoice always, pray without ceasing, and be thankful in all things. These very directives that are *humanly* impossible possess a beautiful potential through the moment-by-moment connection of God's Spirit with our heart and mind.

If you are a believer, He has taken up residence within you. (You are the temple in which His Spirit dwells, remember?) You are permanently plugged in to Him, but like an electric light, you turn on the power as you rejoice and pray and give thanks. We commune with Christ in the endless *now*, the only segment of time we possess and have any control over. Isn't that true? The past is gone; we can't change it. And the future hasn't arrived; we can't predict it. All we have is now. And that's all God asks for. Our now.

Let's analyze this a little further. Scripture says, "Pray without ceasing." How do we do that? By consciously focusing on Christ from the moment we wake in the morning. We acknowledge His presence. We thank Him for another day and invite Him to guide us. We share with Him our needs and ask for His strength to face whatever comes.

As the day progresses, we keep a running conversation going with the Lord. We keep an attitude of gratitude, thanking Him for our food as we eat, for the beautiful day as we drive to work. As we interact with others, we ask God to bless them through us. As we do our job, we entreat God to help us. As anger rises or temptation strikes, we cry out to God for grace to overcome.

Wives, even when you are spending intimate moments with your husband, ask God to help you show that dear man how much you love him. God wants you to love your husband passionately, with delicious abandon. You please God when you do so, not to mention pleasing your husband, and maybe even yourself as well. You may be saying, "Oh, I don't think God would be interested in that aspect of my life." Wouldn't He? What did He say about counting the hairs of your head? There's nothing in our lives God can't help us with . . . or make better. Everything's better with God!

When your kids are driving you up the wall, entreat God for a hefty helping of His love and wisdom. When you abide in an attitude of prayer, you see things from God's viewpoint. It's difficult to hold a grudge against someone you're praying for.

Let God
Turn Your
Negative
Self-Talk
into "Divine
Dialogues"
with Him

Some people say God seems far away when they pray. Why? Because they haven't carried on a running conversation with Him. Keep thoughts of Him simmering on the back burner of your mind. Be sensitive to His murmuring whispers in your heart. Communing with Him throughout your day imbues even the most ordinary and tedious activities with a significance they otherwise wouldn't hold. Even washing dishes or scrubbing a floor can be a spiritual event if our mind is stayed on Christ.

Please burn this truth on your heart and mind: God wants us to have a lifelong love relationship with Him. He wants us to feel the surge of love and impassioned response that honeymooners feel. We yearn to be in our bridegroom's presence. We can't get enough of him. We want to tell him everything and share everything with him.

It's the same way with Christ. We confess our transgressions the moment we're aware of them so that guilt doesn't drive a divisive wedge between us. We feel energized and empowered by Christ's love, as if we could do anything, be anything. And we see the world through the filter of His love so that life is suffused with a beauty we never experienced before.

As improbable as it may sound, we have the potential of living life this way, in a perpetual "honeymoon" with Christ, as we abide in His all-encompassing love. We begin by training our self-talk to include God until it becomes natural for us, a true divine dialogue. Communing with Him becomes as instinctive and necessary as breathing, as we make ourselves vulnerable to Him and candidly reveal our thoughts, feelings, and needs as they occur.

This process of communing with God on a moment-by-moment basis helps us to step back and see our life through Christ's eyes. It gives us constant snapshots of our unique world—a godly perspective, an eternal glimpse, much like Emily was given in the play *Our Town*. Remember her? After her death, she goes back and sees her life from a new and timeless perspective that helps her appreciate the most ordinary details and the most mundane moments with those she loved. Living the moment with Christ helps us to do the same thing while we're alive.

So do it!

Live the moment with Christ!

Keep your heart and mind in an attitude of prayer, rejoicing, and thanksgiving. Maybe this is what Paul meant in Romans 12:2, when he urged, "And do not be conformed to this world, but be transformed by the renewing of your mind, that you may prove what is that good and acceptable and perfect will of God."

One final thought while we're on this subject. Scientists have proven that there's a relationship between our thought patterns and the physical condition of our brain. Negative thinking has a negative effect on the brain, while positive thinking has a positive physical impact. Hence, Scripture passages that urge us to "rejoice always, pray without ceasing, and in everything give thanks" are not just spiritually sound; they're also good for our mental health. They actually make our brain better. So if we choose to stew in our own negative juices rather than taking our troubles promptly to Christ and receiving His love, peace, and joy, we could be "cooking our own goose" health-wise.

TAKING ACTION

I'd like to conclude this chapter with some practical suggestions for channeling our self-talk into positive action. Many of us live our lives like a person floating on his back in the sea, going wherever the waves take him. He mindlessly drifts here and there without a thought or a plan, simply taking up space and killing time. He never reaches his destination, because he never set his sights on one. He's content to roll along in a dazed, complacent stupor.

Compare this lackadaisical fellow to the man who desires to make the Olympic swim team. He knows exactly what he must do and how he must prepare and then trains vigorously for months or years, often at great personal sacrifice. His goal is never far from his mind. It impacts everything he does.

Which one do you most resemble? The fellow floating aimlessly on his back or the Olympic swimmer gearing up for the big challenge? Or maybe, like me, you consider yourself somewhere between the two.

So what can we do to get ourselves moving?

Enter the race. Hebrews 12:1–2 tells us, "Let us run with endurance the race that is set before us, looking unto Jesus, the author and finisher of our faith, who for the joy that was set before Him endured the cross." We can begin by letting Jesus be our example. He came to do the Father's will, and He didn't stop until He declared in a loud voice on the cross, "It is finished!"

Catch the vision. We need to catch the vision of what God wants us to do. Proverbs 29:18 tells us, "Where there is no vision, the people perish" (kjv). What is your vision for the work God wants you to do? Can you state your vision, your life's goal, in a simple declarative sentence? My ministry goal is a three-pronged vision: to write the books God calls me to write, to mentor and instruct other writers, and to speak to women's groups about becoming women of passion for Christ.

Don't make excuses. It's so easy to make excuses as to why we aren't doing the work God has called us to do. Yes, we live busy lives. No doubt your schedule is filled with all sorts of activities from morning until night. But are you doing something that nurtures your vision? Or are you too busy fulfilling other people's agendas? If so, remember these two words: Set priorities.

I was a young wife and mother with a toddler and a new baby at home when I sold my first story to a Sunday school take-home paper thirty years ago. In those days, because my children were little and my family came first, I was fortunate if I managed to grab a few hours a week to write. It felt like a huge accomplishment to complete half a dozen short stories a year. But even though I was taking the tiniest baby steps those first few years, I was applying myself to the vision God had given me. Year after year, God afforded me more time for my writing and teaching ministry. And now today, with my children grown, I'm able to work full-time at writing, speaking, and teaching.

Focus on a specific target. You'll never hit a target you can't see clearly, and you'll never hit higher than you aim. I learned in a college archery course that the trajectory of an arrow in flight requires the archer to aim his arrow even higher than the bull's-eye. That's not a bad principle for our lives: Aim higher than the goal you want to reach and chances are you'll hit the bull's-eye.

Persevere. Actor Philip Michael Thomas says, "When you love something enough, it gives up all its secrets." Do you have that kind of passion to stick with something until you've discovered its secrets? If I had to pick one single trait that spells the difference between failure and success, it's perseverance.

Set workable goals. Psychologist Charles Garfield says, "Goals are dreams with deadlines." What are your dreams? How are you turning them into reachable goals? Ask yourself, "What can I do today to begin accomplishing my goal?" Even if you set aside only fifteen minutes a day for your dream, in a year you'll feel as though you've accomplished something significant.

Some women write out mission statements listing the specific tasks they believe God has called them to do. Writing down your goals gives them a validity and con-

LET GOD
TURN YOUR
NEGATIVE
SELF-TALK
INTO "DIVINE
DIALOGUES"
WITH HIM

creteness they rarely have if merely flittering around in your mind like confetti. Exploring ways you can turn your dreams into achievable goals and committing them to paper sharpen your mental skills. Prayerfully write down what you believe God wants you to accomplish in a week, a month, a year, five years, and by the end of your life. Save this unofficial contract. Put it in a special place. Take it out often and read it again to see how you're doing. It'll help keep you on track, and before you know it you'll see those elusive dreams turning into solid accomplishments.

Step out of your comfort zone. At some point we need to be willing to step out of our comfort zone to embrace the work God has called us to do. Personal and spiritual growth come as we make ourselves available to God in new, untried areas. If you find yourself feeling entirely comfortable with your present endeavors, chances are you are missing rare and wonderful opportunities to let God demonstrate His magnitude and diversity through you. Garrisoned with prayer, risk exploring new worlds of service and untraveled avenues of ministry. And brace yourself for all the surprising and marvelous ways God will use you.

A TIME FOR REFLECTION

1. Think about the self-talk that has occupied your mind in recent weeks. Is any of it negative? Where did it come from? Do you hear a specific critical voice from your past? Whose? What effect has your negative self-talk had on your attitude toward yourself? On your emotions? On your actions?

2. Spend time in prayer today asking God to help you turn your negative self-talk into divine dialogues with Him. Think about how much He loves you and wants to be involved in your life. (He's even counted the hairs of your head.) Ask God to reveal new ways you can serve and honor Him amid your

daily activities. Invite Him to show you new horizons He wants you to explore.

 *A Time for Action*

1. Take out your journal and list three negative statements your self-talk is telling you. (For example, "I feel guilty for all the wrong things I've done. I don't have what it takes to keep up with my busy schedule. I'll never get a promotion because I'm not as smart as everyone else.")

   Now, beside each negative statement write down the positive response the Holy Spirit might prompt within you. (For example, "If I confess my sins, God is faithful to forgive my sins. I can do all things through Christ, who strengthens me. God can equip me for whatever task He calls me to do.")

2. Write down and memorize 1 Thessalonians 5:16–18. Every day repeat these verses to yourself until they become second nature to you. Practice turning your negative self-talk into divine dialogues with Christ by disciplining your mind to "rejoice always, pray without ceasing, and in everything give thanks." Think it's too hard? Then read the last part of verse 18: "For this is the will of God in Christ Jesus for you." Just as we may have conditioned our minds to think negatively, so we can condition them to respond with prayer, praise, and joy.

3. In your journal prayerfully write down your goals for the future. These may include personal, spiritual, marital, financial, professional, and family goals. Then divide your goals into workable segments, listing for each goal what you want to accomplish within a year, five years, ten years, by the end of your life. (For example, "By the end of the year I want to be having consistent family devotions. I want to join a women's Bible study. I want to pay off my student

loan. I want to establish Friday night dates with my husband. I want to return to teaching when my children are in school.")

4. We can change our self-talk. We can set goals to make changes in our daily lives. But part of having a healthy mind is realizing that there are some things in life we cannot change. The wise woman knows the difference between what can be changed and what cannot.

Write in your journal, describing those things in your life that hold the potential for change and those that do not. Keep in mind that sometimes even what can't be changed can be improved upon with love, prayer, and diligence. Can you think of any such instances in your own home or family? Write them down.

Here are some examples: Your husband has diabetes, which you can't change. But you can find ways to improve his diet and join him in exercise to improve his general health. You can't change the fact that your son or daughter made wrong choices that brought deep pain to your family. But you can control the way you respond to your child by exhibiting godly forgiveness and unconditional love.

PART TWO

Keep Passion Alive on the Home Front

A Woman of Passion Nurtures Loving Intimacy with Those in Her Circle of Love

8

Love Others out of an Overflow of God's Love

 The first time I encountered Tara at my sister-in-law's house, it was love at first sight. My husband, Bill, was equally smitten. Tara was willowy and sleek and had the most luxurious platinum blonde hair I'd ever seen. And when she looked at us with those huge, wistful brown eyes, our hearts melted.

If Marilyn Monroe had been a dog, she would have looked exactly like Tara. Graceful and lean, Tara was a pedigreed afghan with the long legs and aristocratic snout to match.

And she needed a home.

Our niece Karen, who worked for a veterinarian, had rescued Tara when her owner brought her in to be put to sleep. Tara had been a show dog until she had broken her leg, and now her owner didn't want her. So Karen took

Tara home, intending to breed her, until she was told afghans were too temperamental.

Then, when Tara clashed with Karen's other dogs, Karen had no choice but to find Tara another home. And so she brought the flaxen afghan to her mom's house, where Bill and I first saw her.

Now, before I go on with my story, I should make something absolutely clear. Bill and I are not pet people, although we've had our share—a goldfish, a rat, a chicken, two rabbits, a cat, and (counting Tara) a dog (not all at once, thank goodness!). So we weren't in the market for an animal of any kind.

But when we saw Tara, it was as if lightning had struck. Or maybe Cupid's arrow. We both knew immediately that Tara was going to be ours. And the way she nuzzled us and gazed up trustingly with those enormous mahogany peepers, we could tell the feeling was mutual. That very evening we took her home.

To be honest, at that time we didn't know the first thing about dogs. For instance, what do you do when you take home a dog the size of a small horse who struts around like royalty and doesn't seem to know she's a dog? You do the only thing you can do: You give her full reign of the house, which she promptly took over without batting her long dark eyelashes!

Tara had no interest in sleeping on the floor. No, she was quite comfortable stretching out full-length on my good sofa, thank you very much. Then one morning I entered my teenage son's room and stared in shock at his sofa bed. My innocent baby boy was sleeping with a blonde. When I looked closer, I realized it was Tara under the covers beside David, her blonde head comfortably ensconced on the pillow next to his.

When Tara came to live with us, she was thin and undernourished, so we quickly set out to fatten her up. As the weeks passed, I marveled at what a good job we were doing. Tara was no longer the scrawny animal we had originally taken under our roof. No, siree! She was filling out beautifully.

Then one day as I was sitting on the sofa reading, I reached down to Tara beside me and rubbed her tummy. Something moved. I jumped, startled, and felt again, pressing my hand gently on her warm fur. More strange little movements. No, it wasn't possible! Surely she couldn't be pregnant. She hadn't been near another dog since we'd brought her home. And Karen's words reassuringly echoed in my mind: "Afghans are too temperamental to breed."

But something was up. I knew the rumbling in her stomach wasn't gas. I phoned everyone I knew who had ever had a dog, and I got the same advice: Just in case, make up a bed for Tara in the garage.

That evening Bill and I did just that. I could tell Tara wasn't happy being banished to the garage and trading her comfy sofa for a makeshift bed on the cold cement. But I quelled my guilt feelings and went to bed.

Toward morning I awoke. I had heard something, a faint, distant commotion. Bill and I jumped out of bed and hurried out to the garage to find Tara nursing her babies. That night she delivered eight darling little coal-black puppies. (We later learned she had had a fling with a black German shepherd next door to Karen. So much for afghans being too temperamental to make whoopee!)

So Bill and I—who had never wanted a dog—ended up with nine dogs. We eventually found homes for all the puppies, but we kept Tara, who lived to a ripe old age (in dog years). We'll never forget her. She was a one and only original.

So what's the point of my story?

When you fall in love with something (or someone), you never know what you're going to get. We got nine in one.

What about you?

What did you fall in love with?

And were you surprised with what you got?

In this section we're going to talk about keeping passion alive on the home front. Your home front may include a husband and children, or just the kids, or maybe parents, or other relatives, or friends. Every home is different. And yet we all have something in common: the challenge of getting along with the other people in our lives.

I'm going to be talking a lot about marriage and parenthood, but if you're a single woman, please don't tune me out. The principles for getting along with a husband and children are essentially the same for all our relationships. So we're going to be exploring ways to maximize our understanding and compassion for those in our circle of love, whoever they may be.

Passion on the Home Front

I'm sure you realize by now I'm not a marriage counselor or a psychologist. But I am a wife, mother, grandmother, and friend. All I can do is share with you what I've learned during thirty-four years of living contentedly and at peace with the same man. We've raised three children. Heather, our youngest, is in college. Our son, David, and older daughter, Kimberle, are happily married and raising families of their own. Praise God, all our children and their spouses are committed to Christ and raising their children in the church.

Maybe you're assuming I knew from the beginning what I was doing when it came to love and marriage. Hate to burst your bubble.

I admit, when I was young and single, I knew exactly what kind of man I wanted to marry. He would be a tender, gentle, sensitive, romantic man, an artist at heart, and a writer too, a poet—yes, he would write deep, magnificent poetry that would convince me he was "the one" because he could read my very soul.

He would love to sit by my side and critique my writings, and because he was such a deep literary thinker, we would spend our leisurely hours discussing Dylan Thomas and T. S. Eliot. He would love art and music too and enjoy escorting me to local art museums, stage plays, and concerts. He would have an amazing singing voice, and, just for fun, we would sing duets together as we walked along the beach in the moonlight. And being a devout Christian with a deep knowledge of Scripture, he would astonish me with his vast wisdom and perceptive insights.

Then along came Bill.

Bill hates to read, especially poetry. He wouldn't know a poem from a Popsicle. He loves music but can't warble a note. Bill is a stubborn, practical, hardworking, no-nonsense, take-charge aerospace engineer—sensible, logical, dependable, down to earth. He's an expert at checking drawings of aircraft and missiles. But he's the exact opposite of everything I thought I wanted in a man.

And my opposite in nearly every way. While I'm naturally reticent and an introvert at heart, Bill is outgoing and friendly and totally at ease with people in any situation. And he possesses a delightful dry wit that keeps me on my toes.

As we dated, I discovered that where I was weak, Bill was strong, and vice versa. I could count on him. He was solid as a rock, not flighty and whimsical like my imaginary poet. I loved his strength, his boldness and tenacity, his honesty and integrity. I loved the way he treated his mother. I admired his unwavering commitment to God and the way he practiced his faith in simple, everyday ways. He rarely missed a church service, was quick to help a friend, and tithed his income faithfully. He was kind, generous, and genuine.

And I soon knew he was the man God wanted for me. I was living in California at the time, half a continent away from my family in Michigan, and yet, with Bill, I felt as if I had finally come home. Today, I often quip that Bill and I together make one whole person. He keeps me down to earth; I help him soar a little. Isn't that the way it's supposed to be? Bill still doesn't read my manuscripts, but with his constant encouragement and steadfast support, he has helped me in countless ways become the person—and the writer and teacher—I am today.

Wives, I wish I could hear your story of how you and your husband met and fell in love. I'd love to hear of the discoveries you've made about each other, about marriage, and about life with all its surprises and mysteries and struggles and ironies.

I think there's one thing we can agree on. A good relationship doesn't just drop into our lap. Nor does a good marriage happen by accident. It takes a lot of care and nourishing and plain hard work.

What advice does Scripture give husbands and wives? Paul had some extraordinary things to say, concepts that are considered controversial in many circles today.

Let's take a look at Ephesians 5:22–33:

> Wives, submit to your own husbands, as to the Lord. For the husband is head of the wife, as also Christ is head of the church; and He is the Savior of the body. Therefore, just as the church is subject to Christ, so let the wives be to their own husbands in everything. Husbands, love your wives, just as Christ also loved the church and gave Himself for it, that He might sanctify and cleanse it with the washing of water by the word, that He might present it to Himself a glorious church, not having spot or wrinkle or any such thing, but that it should be holy and without blemish. So husbands ought to love their own wives as their own bodies; he who loves his wife loves himself. For no one ever hated his own flesh, but nourishes and

cherishes it, just as the Lord does the church. For we are
members of His body, of His flesh and of His bones. "For
this reason a man shall leave his father and mother and
be joined to his wife, and the two shall become one flesh."
This is a great mystery, but I speak concerning Christ and
the church. Nevertheless let each one of you in particular so love his own wife as himself, and let the wife see
that she respects her husband.

You can see Paul had strong opinions about the roles
of husbands and wives. Okay, so Paul wouldn't fly on
Oprah these days; he'd be branded a male chauvinist pig
and be banished to some obscure station on late-night
TV. But if you take another look at what he's actually saying, you'll see the splendor of truth in his words.

Do you notice in this passage how often Paul tells husbands to love their wives? Three times in a few short paragraphs. Paul even tells husbands *how* they should love
their wives . . . as their own bodies and as Christ loved
the church and gave Himself for it. Do you get that? Paul
is telling our husbands they're supposed to love us with
the same love they have for themselves . . . and more!
Much more! They're to love us with the same kind of love
Christ has for us, love so vast and unbounded that our
husband would be willing to die for us. Wow! That's a tall
order, isn't it? (Especially if your husband doesn't even
want to share the remote control.)

If I were writing this book for husbands, I could wax
eloquent on the subject of their sacrificial love. I could
let them have it with both barrels. I could harp for the
next twenty pages about all they should be doing to show
us they love us with Christ's love.

But I'm not writing to our husbands. There's nothing I
can say in this book to change our husbands. How well
they exemplify the love principle of these Scripture verses
is between them and God. The people I'm intent on changing are . . . you and me, dear sister. We can't change our

husbands, but we can change some things about ourselves that may indirectly influence our husbands' behavior.

Do you wonder why Paul doesn't instruct wives to love their husbands? Was it an oversight on his part? I don't think so. Maybe Paul knew it was already in women's nature to love. From the time we hit puberty we're thinking about love. Falling in love, being in love, finding our one true love. Love and romance. That's what marriage is all about for us. So maybe Paul didn't think we needed reminding, since a woman's heart is already programmed for love.

But there were a couple of other things Paul seemed to think we needed to hear, and I agree with his advice, even if it is not considered politically correct today. What did Paul tell us we must do if we're to be godly wives? He said, "Submit to your own husbands, as to the Lord. . . . Just as the church is subject to Christ, so let the wives be to their own husbands in everything. . . . And let the wife see that she respects her husband."

I can already hear the ultrafeminists around us causing an uproar. "Come on, Paul! We're to be subject to our husbands *in everything?* Do you realize what you're saying? What about our right to be independent, self-reliant women? You're taking us back to the Stone Age!"

Paul, of course, knew exactly what he was saying. Marriage isn't simply a contract between two people. It's a commitment between two people . . . and God. God chose marriage to be an illustration of His relationship with the church. He loved us enough to give us everything He had, His very life, and in turn, He asks that we love and serve Him. When we do, we experience His love, joy, and peace.

The principle is much the same in marriage, with one major exception. While Christ is perfect, our husbands aren't. There, I've said it! They're flawed, fallible human beings (sob!). In fact (gasp!), they're downright sinful! To complicate matters even further, we're as sinful as they are!

So how are we supposed to submit ourselves to a guy who doesn't have it together any better than we do? And the kicker is, we're supposed to subject ourselves to him *in everything.* I mean, really, Paul, there's nothing like being totally inflexible, intractable, and unyielding. Lighten up, fella. Couldn't we change "everything" to "a whole lot of things," or "the things we both agree on," or "the things I feel like giving in on"?

And here's another one, Paul. You want us to respect our husbands. Haven't you heard the old saying, "Respect has to be earned"? What do we do if our husband doesn't command our respect?

Respect him anyway.

Paul doesn't give any conditions. But I'll give one, and I think Paul would agree. An abusive husband doesn't deserve respect. He doesn't deserve *you.* Nothing I say in this book should be interpreted to mean you should live with abuse. Don't! Get out. Save yourself. Save your children. God doesn't ask you to accept abuse. He loves you too much for that.

But thank God, most of us don't confront abuse in our homes. Instead, we deal with the daily irritations and annoyances of living with people who are as fallible and unfinished as we are. And hubby may be at the top of the list for exemplifying human frailties.

So how do we show respect for our mere mortal mate who may at times engender more rancor than reverence? We'll get to that in a moment. But first another question: Why should we respect him?

Here's why. A wife's respect is critical for a man's self-esteem. A marriage in which the wife doesn't honor and respect her husband is a troubled union, immensely painful for both partners. Paul knew this truth nearly two thousand years ago. A marriage without respect is a hollow, brittle bond that will produce a nagging, peevish, ridiculing wife and a remote, withdrawn, defeated husband. Paul didn't put it in quite those words, of course, but that's my observation. Our husbands can't thrive without our respect.

Now to the rest of the question. *How* do we respect our husbands? We go back to what Paul said about marriage being an illustration of Christ's relationship with the church.

"Give me a break!" you say. "It's hard enough to muddle through my marriage without worrying about whether it measures up to some lofty ideal like that."

Let's think about this. What we have is a marriage between two imperfect human beings with robust sin natures, and they're trying to exemplify the sacred relationship between Christ and His church. Does that sound like a disaster waiting to happen? It will be, except for one saving grace: the power of Christ to give us godly, supernatural love for one another, love so powerful and all-encompassing that it embraces mutual respect, reverence, and deep regard.

When you get right down to it, here's where the rubber meets the road. The big question! Maybe the only question. How can we love our families and those in our circle of love with that kind of ardor and devotion?

We started out wanting to do just that, didn't we? We vowed to love our mate "till death do us part." (I'm afraid some of us would like to speed that little promise along.) Perhaps the bliss of our honeymoon turned into a bickering inferno. Maybe every conversation has become a heated dispute filled with name-calling and one-upmanship. Perhaps the person you thought would be the answer to your deepest needs is now the source of your greatest pain. All relationships, even with God, will deteriorate if not nurtured and fed by the Spirit.

Lest you think Bill and I have the perfect marriage, let me share with you a few minor anecdotes. Admittedly, not every hour we've spent together has been pure bliss. We've had our moments, especially during our early years together.

There was the time we had a heated argument and in anger I almost jumped out of a moving car. Another time, we stayed up all night trying to roll up our old carpet before the installers arrived the next morning. By dawn we were ready to cancel the new carpet. Why did we need new carpet when we were on the verge of divorce? But we eventually made up, and the carpet looked great.

There was the time, just after Misty died, when Bill and I had a fight, and I ran to the bedroom and slammed the door so hard it stuck. I mean, it wouldn't budge. I tried everything. It was sealed like a bank vault. I finally had to put aside my fury and shout for my husband to come let me out. Imagine my humiliation, begging for a favor when I'd just declared I would never ask him for anything again for the rest of my life. But I had to get out of there someday. After all, I could survive only so long on tap water and toothpaste. Well, Bill was a good sport. He threw his full weight against the door once, twice, three times. Picture the old black-and-white movies in which the good guy charges the locked door until it bursts open. Well, with just a few splinters, our door finally broke open, and, shamefaced, I shuffled out. Within the hour we had made up and would have welcomed a few hours together behind that locked bedroom door.

Okay, I'm not proud of my behavior in these situations. And when my husband finds out I'm even mentioning them to you, he may protest and say it's nobody else's business. And he's right. But the fact remains, if we're going to make this heart journey together, we've got to be honest with ourselves . . . and with one another. I'm sure you wives have stories you could share about the struggles you've faced in your marriage. We need to be honest about what we're like at home. Sometimes we're running on empty, down to the gas fumes.

Author Ethel Barrett says that only by bumping into other people do we develop character.

The classroom for character development is right inside our own home—but we may be flunking out, if:

- we major on the negatives.
- we accumulate grievances.
- we're seasoned critics.

Does that describe us? Always coming up with a critical comeback? Spotting a fault a mile away? Leveling our loved ones with a withering glance, stony silence, or a cold shoulder? If so, what can we do to cure our critical spirit?

We need to begin breaking our negative patterns of reaction and behavior and establish new, positive responses. How? That's the million-dollar question.

THE TRUE SOURCE OF LOVE

We've danced around this subject long enough. Now it's time for some plain talking. What can we as wives do to improve our relationships with our husbands? And for you singles, what can you do to improve your relationships with those in your circle of love?

In the next few chapters, we'll discuss a variety of principles and approaches we can employ to improve family relationships. But all our strategies and tactics begin with the premise of this chapter: Love others out of an overflow of God's love.

Why *His* love? Because the meager human love we generate springs from selfish motives: *I'll love you if you love me. I'll stay with you if you meet all my needs. I'll be true to you as long as you make me happy. When it's no longer good for me, I'll get out.* Tragically, many marriages are based on this me-first principle. No wonder the divorce rate is soaring.

The idea of loving others with godly, unconditional love flies in the face of secular tradition and cultural wisdom. Human nature decries it, logic dismisses it, those espousing the me generation ridicule it.

At the same time, many psychologists today are claiming four main predictors of divorce: contempt, defensiveness, criticism, and withdrawal. In other words, couples most likely to divorce are those who show contempt for each other, are defensive, criticize or disparage one another, especially in front of others, and withdraw emotionally from one another. All of these traits reveal the inadequacy and insufficiency of human love.

What about you? Do you ever feel you're scraping the bottom of the barrel when it comes to loving others?

You've exhausted your inner resources and have no tolerance or compassion left?

You're so thin emotionally you can't summon a modicum of empathy for others?

You just wish everyone would go away and leave you alone for a while?

I confess I'm guilty at times. We're all guilty of such feelings, aren't we?

So how do we get past our own limited stores of love? How do we dip down into the deep, satisfying waters of Christ's love and drink until His compassion flows spontaneously from our lives?

Let's see what Scripture says about love. First John 4:7 and 12 tell us, "Beloved, let us love one another, for love is of God; and everyone who loves is born of God and knows God. . . . If we love one another, God abides in us, and His love has been perfected in us." John 13:34 says, "A new commandment I give to you, that you love one another; as I have loved you, that you also love one another." And Matthew 10:8 admonishes, "Freely you have received, freely give."

The message is clear: Only as God fills us to over-flowing with His limitless love can we freely and abundantly love others.

Think of situations at home that prompt hurt feelings or anger. You fix a great dinner, and your husband's a no-show. He belittles you where you're most vulnerable. He doesn't seem to need or appreciate the best qualities you have to give. He doesn't really look at you or talk to you anymore.

Or your housemate or best friend doesn't have time for you lately. She says she's too busy for a special lunch out, then you see her lunching with a mutual friend.

Or a colleague is trying to sabotage your new promotion.

Or a relative is spreading rumors about you to other family members.

How should we respond to these kinds of behavior? I'll tell you. This may sound revolutionary, preposterous, unthinkable. But it works. Respond directly to Christ and indirectly to others. How?

- By spending time in Christ's presence, praying, studying, and memorizing His Word.
- By revealing our most intimate selves fully and freely to Christ.
- By confessing our sins and expressing our needs, hopes, and desires to the Lord.
- By sharing with Christ all that is important to us and giving Him time to work in our hearts.
- By telling Christ we love Him, enjoying His presence, and basking in His love.
- By going out and responding to others from a heart overflowing with Christ's love.

How does this work in the real world, responding directly to Christ and indirectly to others?

Let's look at a specific scenario. Your husband promises to take you out to dinner tonight to your favorite restaurant. It's going to be expensive, but it's worth it, because this is going to be a night to remember, a night to recapture the romance of your youth. As you spend the day getting ready, you play out every detail of the evening in your imagination. Your anticipation grows. You can't wait. But that afternoon your dear husband calls and tells you his best buddy dropped into town and has tickets for the ball game, so naturally he has to go. "Sorry, darling," he says. "We'll have to postpone our night out. You understand, don't you? We can always eat out, but I can't always get together with Bob and the guys."

What would your natural reaction be?

Boil that boy in oil!

Okay, we agree you'll be wrestling with plenty of anger, frustration, and disappointment. While you're waiting for him to come home, you do a slow boil, and when he walks in the door, you explode. "You selfish jerk! How dare you cancel our date and go out with the guys? Don't you ever think of anybody but yourself? What about my feelings? Don't they count for anything? I should have known better than to marry the likes of you!"

You can be sure the evening is going to heat up now, not with romance, but with more hot, blistering accusations and bitter recriminations. It could even lead to a knockdown, drag-out fight, with hubby sleeping on the couch and you in bed alone, crying yourself to sleep.

Not a pretty picture, is it?

How could we have handled this differently? By responding *first* to Christ and *then* to our oblivious hubby-in-the-doghouse, we can break the negative pattern of bickering, brawls, and battles.

Let's rewind the videotape and take another look at how we might have handled our thoughtless, insensitive mate. First, we must go back to that moment when he breaks the date. We're too stunned to respond, so we hang up the phone with only a curt good-bye. Now what? We can wallow in outrage and self-pity until we've immersed ourselves in the dark, miry waters of bitterness and indignation.

Or . . . we can take our expectations to Christ and leave them with Him. We might say something like this: "Lord, You know how much I was counting on tonight. It's been so long since John and I spent quality time together. You know how angry I am and how much I want to strike back. I want to make him hurt the way he's hurting me. I can't love him in my own strength, Father. I give to You my dashed hopes and shattered dreams, all my plans and expectations. I am Yours, Lord. Take my disappointment and anger and let Your Spirit fill me with Your love, joy, and peace. Give me the words to say to make my husband understand how much I need and love him. Turn this ruined evening into a chance for John and me to grow closer and understand each other better."

After spending a prayerful evening in the presence of Christ, how do you suppose you'll greet your wayward spouse? Not with heated words and a raised baseball bat, I'm sure.

Your response will be filtered through Christ's love. Because your neediness has already been met by His ministering Spirit, you will be able to greet your husband with honesty, loving concern, and a willingness to discuss the situation calmly. You might say something like this: "Dear, I know you need time with your friends, and I want you to have that time. But I need time with you too. Maybe I haven't made that clear enough before. To be honest, I was really hurt and angry when you canceled our plans. Our date tonight was very important to me. I feel we've been drifting apart, and I thought spending some quality time together would bring us closer. While you were gone I spent some time praying. God healed my anger and reminded me how much I love you. I still want that special date with you. What about tomorrow night?"

See how it works? You express your needs honestly but without bitterness and resentment. By immersing yourself in Christ's love and letting that love overflow to your husband, you've broken the destructive cycle of rage, wrath, and wrangling.

If we respond to others with lovingkindness, they will have to come up with a new reaction to us, thus setting in motion a whole new set of responses. This doesn't mean you should be a doormat and let people walk all over you. No way! You boldly speak the truth in love.

Remember Jesus' words in Matthew 10:8: "Freely you have received, freely give." The love we have received from Christ we are to give freely to others, especially to our families. It begins with one person recognizing that all our needs and expectations can be met in Jesus Christ.

Some might argue, "But where's the justice? The wife is just giving in to her selfish husband. How is that fair? Doesn't she know that being submissive to her husband is a negative, old-fashioned concept?"

Is it?

Norm Wright says, "A wife's submission to her husband is from complete freedom and love, not from compulsion or fear. The Church submits to the Lordship of Christ on a voluntary basis—in response to His love. The wife's motivation in submitting to her husband should be the same."[1]

The biblical principle is that we as wives choose to submit to our husbands, not because they threaten or demand that we do so, but because our voluntary compliance reflects the church's submission to Christ. Submission does not mean subservience but rather quietly recognizing our husband's role of leadership in the home. The model is not a husband wielding his power like some bellowing, chest-pounding Tarzan but rather a wife showing her strength of spirit by willingly honoring her husband's God-given position.

The concept of the submissive wife should never summon images of a woman being browbeaten, disparaged, or repressed. It should never involve physical, mental, or emotional abuse. Nor should she feel she must relinquish her wishes and opinions or stifle her unique personhood. But just as the church is most healthy and whole and joyous when it submits to Christ, so is the wife who lovingly defers to her husband as unto the Lord.

 *A Time for Reflection*

1. Wives, think about ways you and your husband are alike. In what ways are you opposites (aside from the obvious)? How do your similarities and differences affect your relationship, in both positive and negative ways? How can you bring greater harmony to your relationship?

2. Wives, do you find it difficult to submit to your husband? Why or why not? In what ways could you reinforce his role as head of the home? Are there areas of discord or dissension that prevent you from recognizing his position of leadership? What steps can you take to eliminate the friction between you?

3. Singles, think about your most significant relationships. How can the principle of responding directly to Christ and indirectly to others impact these relationships in a positive way? If you have housemates, how do the principles of submission, responsibility, and respect enter in, especially concerning the division of chores, respecting one another's property and privacy, and living in harmony in spite of differing opinions and agendas?

 # A Time for Action

1. Write freely in your journal describing your relationship with your husband, both the positives and the negatives. List troubled areas and ways they could be improved. Are there issues you personally need to resolve regarding your husband? Prayerfully invite God to give you insights into yourself, your husband, and your relationship.

2. Wives, write a love letter to your husband, telling him all the things about him you love and admire. In your own words, let him know you want to be available to support and encourage him as he becomes the man God wants him to be. Tell him how thankful you are for him and mention his special accomplishments and qualities you adore. Close the letter by asking him what you can do today to show him Christ's abundant love. (This letter will be effective only if you actually give it to your husband. You notably passionate wives may want to write your letter on perfumed stationery and leave it on his pillow tonight.)

3. For those of you who are not married, write in your journal about an especially trying relationship that needs the touch of God's love. Ask Christ to make you the emissary of His love to that person. Make a list of ways you can show loving concern. Seek an opportunity to clear the air, apologize if necessary, and resolve hurtful feelings. If you can't talk face to face, write a letter sharing your heart and expressing your love.

9
NURTURE TENDER
INTIMACY WITH
THOSE YOU LOVE

In the last chapter I told you my dog story. Now I want to tell you my cat story. This one's a tad painful to tell.

You already know Bill and I aren't exactly pet people. We didn't want a dog, but we got nine in one. We don't especially like dogs, but we loved Tara. Well, if we aren't all that fond of dogs, we positively loathe cats. Bill especially. (Okay, you cat lovers, before you slam this book shut, let me clarify my position here. When I was a child I adored cats. Wanted one so badly I pretended a stuffed one was real. Took it everywhere I went. I still think cats are gorgeous creatures. But if I get too close to one, I sneeze like crazy, my eyes swell, and my head feels like a balloon. So the furry little creatures don't exactly endear themselves to me anymore. Am I off the hook?)

Okay, here's the story.

Some years ago, while she was still single, our older daughter, Kimberle, was living on her own. (In most families the kids grow up and leave home. In our family the kids grew up and *Bill and I* left home. We moved an hour away, and since Kim and our son, David, didn't want to go, Kim moved in with friends and David took up residence in a Christian fraternity house.) At this time Kimberle, a graceful, willowy charmer studying theater at Long Beach State University, was in what we called her "black phase." Every item of clothing she owned was black, a stunning contrast to her flowing blonde hair and expressive mahogany-brown eyes.

About a year after Bill and I moved into our new house, Kimberle packed her belongings and came home, bringing her beloved cat in her arms—an outdoor tomcat named Kitty. That's right. Kitty. Kitty Cat. We told Kim she was welcome to stay. But not the cat.

They both moved in anyway—our daughter in black with her cat. A few months later Kim moved out and left us the cat. We hated this cat more than ever. It roamed the neighborhood at night, fought with other cats, and snuck through our neighbors' cat doors and ate their cats' food. One neighbor even woke up one night and found our cat in bed with her! She wasn't amused.

One night another neighbor—a devoted cat lover—knocked on my door with Kitty in his arms. He told me our cat had been in a fight with another cat and needed immediate medical attention. Kitty did look a bit scruffy but not seriously injured. But then what did I know about the feline species? And if my neighbor felt he needed treatment, who was I to argue? Only one problem. Bill was working out of town and had our only car. So Kitty's medical treatment would have to wait a few hours.

When Bill finally arrived home late that night (about 11:00 P.M.), exhausted after a two-hour commute, I broke the news that Kitty had been in a fight and we needed to take him to the vet. You would think I had announced the end of life on this planet as we know it. Bill exploded. After combating two hours of heavy freeway traffic, he wasn't about to venture out for a cat he didn't want in the first place.

"We've got to," I said, "or we'll be guilty of cruelty to animals."

That obviously wasn't the right thing to say, because Bill's face turned beet red, he glowered at me as only Bill can glower, and I could have sworn I saw storm clouds gathering around his head. "Come on!" he said, and tramped back out to the car. So Heather, our youngest, about nine at the time, who utterly adored Kitty, piled in the backseat with the cat in her lap, and I got in beside my seething hubby.

There was only one problem. No veterinarian was open at that time of night. The only place open was an animal hospital many, many miles away in another city.

So we ventured out into the night, Bill grumbling and complaining, Heather bawling, the cat scratching and clawing to get free, and me biting my tongue to keep from screaming from frustration.

Our motley little menagerie promptly got stuck in bumper-to-bumper traffic inching at a snail's pace, the result of a fender bender up the road. The louder Bill complained, the more silent I grew, my stomach clenching in knots.

By midnight we arrived at the animal hospital, all of us looking more weary and bedraggled than our feisty, cantankerous Kitty. We collapsed in straight-back chairs in the tiny waiting room while an attendant whisked Kitty off to an examining room. After several interminable hours of waiting, the veterinarian appeared and, with a placid smile, handed us our cat. Sure enough, Kitty was on the mend, his leg in a splint.

The vet also handed us a small pharmacy of cat medicine with incomprehensible instructions . . . and (groan, gulp, grumble) he handed Bill a hefty bill! (If we'd known the high cost of medical treatment for animals, we'd have taken out Blue Cross on Kitty. There's Medicare. What about Pet-a-care?)

All the way home Bill complained, "Why should I pay all this money for a cat I never wanted—and still don't want!"

All night we fussed with that cat, coaxing, coddling, pleading, wheedling, but nothing would persuade Kitty to take his medicine.

The next morning I had to teach a class at Biola University, over an hour away, so I asked Bill to give the cat his medicine. You would think I had asked him to give up a kidney. The cat complaints began all over again. I couldn't take it. I had kept my mouth shut for the past twenty-four hours while Bill ranted and raved. Now I'd had enough. I ran upstairs to the bedroom and slammed the door (not *too* hard—I had learned my lesson on that one!).

I kept thinking, *I could just scream!* And then I thought, *Why not?*

So for the first and only time in my life, I just opened my mouth and let it rip. Yep, I screamed like a banshee. Loud enough to shake the rafters. I mean, I let it out, loud and long, with full vibrato!

Bill and Heather came bounding up the stairs and into the bedroom, their eyes wide as saucers, scared out of their wits, convinced I'd finally snapped and lost my blooming mind. I hadn't. Or that I was having a heart attack. I wasn't.

I just felt like screaming.

And that's how a tomcat named Kitty almost cost me my happy home.

(Just in case you're wondering where the story goes from there, we gave the cat back to Kim, and she later fell in love with Jay, another cat lover. They got married and set up their household with their two beloved cats, his and hers. Meanwhile, Bill and I resumed our happy marriage, totally cat-free.)

Maybe you have a cat story too. Not like mine. But one of your own. Maybe without a cat. But the rest of the ingredients are there—a crisis situation that strikes at the heart of your peaceful home and leaves you warring with those you love most. Trying circumstances that make you want to scream. Maybe, like me, you did scream.

I've shared my cat story because I want you to know, as much as I would love to live in an ideal home with perfect people, a place where everyone gets along 100 percent of the time and no one ruffles anyone else's feathers, it simply isn't so. My home is like yours; my family is like your family. And I bet I'm a lot like you. Not a carbon copy, of course. But there are enough similarities in our lives that I think we probably face many of the same problems and challenges. And unfortunately, we're just as imperfect as the rest of our clan.

We all have issues and aggravations in our lives that bring us to the breaking point. How do *you* handle the conflicts, irritations, and disputes in your home? Sometimes we focus so much on the problems and annoyances that we overlook the glimmers of hope and fragile rays of sunshine winging through the darkness.

RUN TO JESUS

Before we talk about ways to nurture tender intimacy with those we love, we need to figure out what to do with all the petty gripes and grievances we accumulate from day to day. Let's face it, in an ordinary day we can come up with a bushelful, right? How can we nurture loving intimacy with someone we want to hit with a broom or kick out on his or her derriere?

What do we do when our daily stress level gets too high, when we find ourselves tempted to sling harsh words at our mate or give our children a one-way ticket to Siberia or barricade ourselves in the walk-in closet until everyone goes away? Do we just grin and bear it? Do we strengthen our vocal cords so we can outlast them in a shouting match? Do we chalk up our frustrations as the price we pay for wanting a family in the first place? (Who knew we'd end up with such a curious collection of uncommonly odd individuals?) Do we throw up our hands in despair? Or scrape the bottom of our emotional barrel for a few dregs of affection to cast at our irksome brood?

The solution to our mounting stress is found in what we talked about in the last chapter, the principle of responding directly to Christ and indirectly to others, of finding our needs met in Him so we can love others out of an overflow of His love.

I want to elaborate on this idea, because it is such a powerful concept. And yet we can so easily miss the practicality of it. We may agree in theory that it's a nice idea to fill up on Christ's love and let it overflow to others, but putting it into practice may be another matter entirely.

Why? Because when we're angry or frustrated or experiencing other negative feelings toward someone, the last thing we want to think about is getting cozy with our heavenly Father.

Ah, have I shocked you? But isn't it true?

In the heat of an argument you're not thinking about prayer, are you? When your husband has said or done something really stupid, something so mean it sets your teeth on edge, you're not in the mood to ask what Jesus would do. When your children have totally blown it and you're wondering how to pick up the pieces, you don't want to serenely let go and let God handle it. When your closest friend lets you down in your moment of greatest need, the last thing you want to show is Christ's forgiving spirit.

No, you want to get in there and grab the situation with both hands and speak your mind and have at it! When conflicts and calamities hit you with both barrels, you just want to nurse your grudges, let your anger fester, and wallow in your misery.

Am I right?

It's not easy changing our reactions from the inside out. It takes supernatural power.

I remember one Christmas a few years ago when the last thing I wanted to do was respond with Jesus' love. It was the Sunday before Christmas, and I was scheduled to have eighteen people over for dinner the next day. At midnight I was still frantically trying to get ready, juggling a million last-minute details, cleaning, decorating, and making sure I had all the ingredients for a sumptuous ham and roast beef dinner. But my mood was anything but merry. In fact, I was silently fuming because I wasn't getting the help I expected from my husband and daughter.

Bill had gone to bed early, even though there was still much to be done. (What could I say? He'd helped out earlier, but that didn't ameliorate my growing self-pity.) A mountain of unwrapped gifts were piled on my kitchen table, and I was wrapping them while Heather stood at the kitchen counter leisurely fixing herself a milk shake while talking on the phone to a friend.

"When are you going to get off that phone and help me?" I snarled. Oh, yes, we were going to have plenty of Christmas spirit at our house!

"In a minute, Mom," she replied and went right on talking as she mixed her shake in the blender.

Then it happened. While balancing the cordless phone against her ear, she tried to pry the top off a whipped cream dispenser. Instead, she slipped and her arm sent the full glass container of milk shake careening off the counter onto the floor. But it didn't just spill. Oh no, that would have been too easy. Rather, the overturned pitcher propelled the thick chocolate shake everywhere in a sticky, gooey ice cream explosion.

Both Heather and I stood there speechless. I stared in shock and dismay at the milk shake streaming across my clean kitchen floor. A fountain of shake had catapulted across the kitchen to the family room and was splattered all over my freshly vacuumed rug and the back of the sofa.

At last I found my voice and started shrieking hysterically for my daughter to do something! But she stood riveted to the spot gazing up at what I hadn't seen yet. The milk shake that had gushed all over my floor and rug and sofa had also shot all over my ceiling and was about to drip on my head.

Do I tell her or wait for her to discover it for herself? my mortified daughter was wondering. I followed her gaze to the ceiling with its oozing globules of shake and couldn't believe my eyes. Eighteen guests coming tomorrow, and milk shake was dripping on my head!

Bill must have heard the commotion because he came to the rescue, and, while I scrubbed the family room carpet, my daughter mopped the kitchen floor and my husband got up on a stool and washed the ceiling. My first impulse was to rant and rave and vent all my outrage. Somewhere amid my waves of frustration, I sent up a weak, halfhearted, "Help me, Lord!" I knew if I spit out all the vituperative accusations churning in my mind, the holiday would be lost, along with my harmonious relationship with my teenage daughter. As we finished cleaning up the mess, I muttered dryly, "Someday I'll laugh about this, but I don't know when."

But surprisingly, by 3:00 A.M., as Heather and I sat wearily wrapping the last of the packages, we both broke into mindless, belly-shaking laughter over the whole incident. We couldn't stop. We laughed and hugged each other and laughed some more.

At dawn, as we dragged ourselves off to bed, even my exhaustion couldn't erase that warm little feeling budding like a fragile flower in my heart. I think they call it Christmas spirit. I was already thanking the Lord that He had given me a double helping of His grace and shown me the humor in a situation that could have spoiled our entire holiday celebration.

Maybe you haven't had to contend with milk shake on your ceiling, but I know you've faced some whoppers in your home. So what do you do when you want to lash out at your loved ones?

> When someone says something to hurt your feelings
>   or does something to belittle or betray you,
> when you feel conflict with someone you love,
> when no one appreciates what you do,
> when circumstances go against you,
> when you lose something or someone precious to you,
> when your natural reaction is anger, bitterness, resentment, depression, or hopelessness . . .

RUN TO JESUS AS FAST AS YOU CAN!

Pour out your heart. As quickly as you can, get alone (lock yourself in the bathroom if necessary) and pour out your heart to your Father God. Be honest. Tell Him exactly how you feel this very moment: "Dear Jesus, no one understands. I feel like I can't go on. How could she do that to me? I'm so angry I want to strike out at someone. I don't even feel like talking to You, God."

Tell God what you need. Tell your loving heavenly Father what your heart yearns for at this moment, the deepest cry of your heart: "Lord, I need Your control, so I don't say something I'll be sorry for. Father, I need a hug. I need to feel appreciated. I need someone to love me. I need encouragement. Lord, I need Your comfort, Your strength, Your help."

Focus on Christ and receive His comfort. Imagine Jesus enfolding you in His arms, drying your tears, whispering His words of consolation. Envision His physical presence and hear His voice in your heart reminding you of His love, whispering, *You are my beloved. I am with you always. I will never leave nor forsake you.*

Surrender yourself to the Holy Spirit. Consciously yield your physical body to God, member by member—head, neck, chest, torso, arms, hands, legs, feet—going slowly from head to toe, until your entire body is relaxed in Him. Surrender your mind, your emotions, your needs, your expectations to the Holy Spirit, releasing everything and relaxing in Him, the way you might lie on your back and float on water, letting the gentle waves carry you where they will.

Praise and worship God. Next, focus all your attention on God. You've mentally stepped outside yourself and your troubling situation; all that matters now is God. Thank Him for whatever happens; praise Him and tell Him you love Him; ask to be conformed to the image of Christ; ask to be used to accomplish God's purpose for you in this situation. Thank Him in advance for what He is going to do.

Return to your world renewed. Return to your situation comforted by Christ, buoyed by His Spirit, physically refreshed, strengthened, and equipped with God's armor, letting Christ's Spirit love and react through you.

Maybe you think what I'm offering here is pie-in-the-sky Pollyanna stuff. Mere sermonizing. A lot of idealistic, fanciful nonsense. I promise you that's not the case. I'm not recommending this process of "running to Jesus as fast as you can" because I think it *might* work. I'm recommending it because I know it *does* work. Jesus has delivered me from countless major and minor crises, from times when I might have said the wrong thing or overreacted or lost my cool. From moments when I felt hopeless, devastated, forsaken, lonely, and misunderstood.

When you follow this step-by-step process of running to Jesus in the midst of trouble, you will discover you feel better, no longer alone, encouraged, calmer, more at peace, ready to face the problem with better perspective and a compassionate heart. And you will be equipped to show the Father's love to your family and those in your circle of love.

Nurturing Tender Intimacy

Now that we've talked about how to handle the negative situations that arise in our daily interactions, let's talk about the positive things we can do to nurture tender intimacy with those in our circle of love.

There's one thing that's easy to do and goes a long way toward creating a loving atmosphere in your home: saying I love you. Some of us wait a lifetime to hear those words. Some of us never hear them. It amazes me how many people say their parents never told them they loved them, over an entire lifetime. How incredibly sad. Those three little words cost so little and accomplish so much. Bill and I always say I love you to each other and to the kids many times a day—out of the blue, at the end of phone conversations, when we part, when we meet, for no reason at all. I love you. How long has it been since you said those crucial words to those you love? Make it a point this week to say I love you to someone at least three times a day. See what a difference it makes.

While we're talking about nurturing intimacy, I want to toss out a few words especially to you wives. (You singles hang in there too. You might find this interesting.) While saying I love you is a great way of expressing how much you care, when it comes to our husbands, they want a whole lot more!

While I don't pretend to be a marriage counselor, I can speak from experience—thirty-four years of marriage to the same man. And because this book is called *Becoming a Woman of Passion,* we can't ignore the role of sexual passion. Let's face it, for our husbands that may be the only definition of passion.

I can see some of you nodding. Maybe you're holding this book in your hands right now because when your husband saw the title he said, "Get it! Get it! You've got to have that book. Here, I'll pay for it myself." And you knew what he was thinking. That this book would make you more passionate in the bedroom.

And I hope it will. Not because I'm going to share with you any marvelous new techniques or revolutionary ideas for lovemaking. This book isn't about hearts and flowers and flickering candles and bubble baths and moonlit strolls and starry nights. Although I'm in favor of all those things if they make your special time together more romantic.

But, wives, let's be candid. Those things are the frosting on the cake. They don't help if there's no cake to slather them on. I believe most problems in the bedroom have nothing to do with the bedroom. They start in our hearts, in our heads. Maybe even in our subconscious minds. Maybe we have no idea what the problem is except that we don't feel that passionate response to our mate anymore. Maybe lovemaking has become more duty than delight, more agony than ecstasy.

I can't address your specific issues, but I can make some general observations based on, as I said, *personal* experience—thirty-four years' worth. Here's what I've noticed. One reason we women don't feel like making

145

mad passionate love is because we've become, uh (I hate to say it), nitpickers.

What's a nitpicker? you ask. According to the dictionary, nits are the eggs of a louse. Louse as in *lice*. The dictionary defines lice as small, flat, wingless, parasitic insects with sucking mouthparts. Honest, I'm not making this up. Pretty repulsive, huh? So then, what is a nitpicker? Someone who picks at nits!

Actually, a nitpicker is someone who pays too much attention to little things, petty details, stuff that shouldn't really matter. Husbands call it "making a big deal about nothing." Shakespeare called it "much ado about nothing."

How does nitpicking "louse" up a marriage? (Excuse the pun; I couldn't resist!) It works like this. In the morning you fix your husband a delicious breakfast, and he sits with his face buried in the newspaper, ignoring you. When he leaves for work—or when you both leave for work—he blows you a kiss that evaporates long before it reaches you. When you call him at work to ask him to pick up the dry cleaning, he's too busy to talk and cuts you off. He comes home without the dry cleaning. He completely forgot. You're both tired from work, but he relaxes in his favorite chair watching TV while you scrounge around in the kitchen for something to eat. After dinner, when you ask him to clear the table, he grumbles about what a hard day he's had.

When you finally collapse into bed beside him that night, he reaches over and pulls you into his arms. He's ready to make whoopee. And you're thinking, *No way!* You draw back, mentally calculating all the times today he has irritated or disappointed you. *Let's see. No conversation, no kiss, abrupt phone call, no dry cleaning, no help in the kitchen.* You've got enough gripes for a bushel basket. You wonder how Mr. Snooze-in-the-Chair can suddenly become so amorous. Doesn't he understand that you're carrying this whole brimming basket of grievances?

Nothing throws a damper on romance faster than nit-picking. And to aggravate the problem, we never let one of those little nits out of our sight, do we? We hold on to every one as if it were gold dust. It's a no-win situation. When we nurse gripes, our resentment quenches whatever ardor we might feel for our mate.

"You mean it's all my fault?" you may ask.

No, I'm not saying that. If I were writing this book for our husbands, I'd tell them, "Hey, wake up, guys! If you want your wife to be more amorous, start courting her in the morning. Show her how special she is. Thank her for the good things she does for you. Kiss her good-bye. Do little favors for her. Sweet-talk her on the phone. Help her in the kitchen. Compliment her. Make her feel cherished before you ever get to the bedroom. Treat her special because she *is* special, not just to get what you want."

I'd say all that and more. But I'm not addressing our husbands. This book is just between us women. And if there's one thing we know, it's that we can't change our husbands. Only the grace of God can change them. That means, if change is going to come, it's got to start with us.

So what do we do? Suppose we relive the day I just outlined, complete with hubby snoozing in the chair while you work; then he rouses to his amorous self when he hits the bed. If you're a first-class nitpicker, you have enough nits to bury him in. In your mind you may experience a general malaise. If your husband asks why you don't feel in a romantic mood, you might not even be able to answer. You don't know why. You're not angry exactly; you just feel a vague displeasure that keeps you from giving yourself wholeheartedly to the moment. Or to him!

Some of us have been nitpicking for so long that we have bushels and bushels of grievances against our husbands. Did you know it's impossible to give yourself freely to your louse, uh, I mean *spouse,* if you're clutching a basket of nitpickings? They get in the way and crowd out tender, loving feelings. They make you hold back, as if to say, *I'll show you. You wouldn't give me what I needed, so I won't give you what you need.*

We're not thinking that consciously, but it's there somewhere, buried under all the nits. The trouble is, we nitpickers hurt ourselves as well as our mate, because those buried resentments turn us off at a subconscious level and extinguish the fires of romance. We gradually grow apart from our spouse and we don't even know why; we just feel an emotional distance that widens day by day until our marriage becomes a hollow shell.

What is the answer?

It's another variation of a familiar theme: Go first to Christ and be filled with His love and then love others out of His abundance.

What is this—a broken record? No, it's not a broken record; it's the way we were programmed by our Creator. His way works. Only His way.

So let's take another look at that fateful day when your husband proves what a turkey he can be. No kiss, no help, no attention, no appreciation. No dry cleaning! He's striking zero.

What do you do? Sulk? Nag? Nitpick?

No. Break the pattern. Try something that works. Sometime during that day, run to Jesus and feast on His love. Let Him fill you to overflowing with the fruits of His Spirit. The nitpicker in you will shrivel and die. No lie! The bushels of nits you've collected will blow away in the refreshing wind of His Spirit. You won't be the same. Your focus will no longer be on your gripes but on God. With His joy and compassion singing in your heart, how can you resist your husband when he needs a touch of your love?

This works. I've tried it. Becoming a woman of passion isn't something we do; it's what we let God do in us. Have you ever asked God to help you love your husband with passionate abandon? It can make all the difference in the world.

Or maybe your problem is that you can't convince yourself God wants you to enjoy sex with your husband. Maybe you can't get past the secret conviction that sex is somehow dirty. It's not surprising you feel that way. Some churches seem to imply that it's sinful to enjoy sex, even in marriage. And you can understand where they're coming from, considering what our culture has done to pervert sex. You see the perversion everywhere—in movies, books, on television, in popular music, on billboards, in magazines. Even the Internet. Everywhere.

Sex is often portrayed as the devil's invention. But he didn't invent it; he polluted it. One of the greatest of human tragedies is that Satan has created the impression that the sexual union is something ugly, smutty, evil. How Satan must laugh with glee at the way he has commandeered sex and made it *his* playground. Not until we step inside heaven's gates and encounter our Savior face to face will we realize what a travesty the world and the devil have made of sex.

For Christian couples to rise above the sick, leering image the world has painted is perhaps a couple's greatest challenge—to make sex the beautiful, giving expression of love and passionate abandon God wants it to be. Our lovemaking is so tainted by our culture's vile portrayal that we as Christian wives may secretly believe there is something dirty or wrong with making love to our husbands. Nothing is farther from the truth.

Sexual passion is a natural, biological drive, programmed within us by our Father God. It was *His* idea. After all, God Himself said, "Be fruitful, and multiply, and replenish the earth. . . . And God saw every thing that He had made, and, behold, it was very good" (Gen. 1:28, 31 KJV). (Read the first chapter of Genesis. Notice that God *spoke* the entire universe into existence with His command, but He formed man *with His own hands* from the dust of the earth and breathed into him the breath of life. We were a hands-on creation, made in God's own image, and He liked what He saw. And what an awesome privilege He gave us—the miracle of sharing with Him in creating human life, for only a man and woman can bring into existence another immortal soul.)

But the devil wants us to focus on the depravity he's made of sex so we'll miss the unique beauty of married love and the exquisite illustration God intended it to be. Christ declared that the physical union between a husband and wife was to represent His love for His church. When is the last time *that* image flitted through your mind while you were being intimate with your mate?

If you want to be reminded of what God has to say about sex, love, and marriage, take some time to read the entire chapter of Ephesians 5. Pay special attention to verses 22–33, preferably reading the passage aloud with your husband.

Paul sets the tone immediately in Ephesians 5, saying we should be imitators of God the way well-loved children imitate their father. We should walk in love, delighting in one another as Christ loved us and gave Himself for us.

But Paul pulls no punches when it comes to taking a stand against immorality. He warns us to have no fellowship with the works of darkness (v. 11), and he concedes it's a shame even to speak of the things such people do in secret (v. 12).

But Paul waxes eloquent when he gets to the subject of husbands and wives. And, of course, his crowning theme is that a married couple's love has a purpose and a resonance far beyond their mutual devotion. Their love is a living, breathing example of Christ's love for the church and the church's love for Christ. Savor the words in this passage and think about their deeper meaning. The purpose of Christ's love was to sanctify us, cleansing us of sin, so that He could present us as His bride in glorious splendor, that we might be holy and faultless before God. Imagine! God uses the marriage of flawed, imperfect people to represent something so incredibly exalted and resplendent.

There you have it. Paul attaches no immorality or impurity to the marital union; far from it! It represents Christ making us His spotless and glorious bride. Think what our marriages could be like if we truly grasped this sublime concept and put it into practice in our homes.

I love what the Amplified Bible does with verse 33. Read it slowly and make it your own personal commitment to your mate.

However, let each man of you (without exception) love his wife as [being in a sense] his very own self; and let the wife see that she respects and reverences her husband— that she notices him, regards him, honors him, prefers him, venerates, and esteems him; and that she defers to him, praises him, and loves and admires him exceedingly.

Whew! A tall order, right? A calling we can fulfill only by God's grace. But the more we respond to the Lover of our souls, the better we will love our all-too-human lover, our mate. If you start today loving your husband out of an overflow of God's love, especially in the bedroom, you will see a transformed husband. I'll go so far as to make a claim that may shock some readers. Nothing makes our husbands happier and more content than being well satisfied in the bedroom.

So go ahead. Light your scented candles, put on the mood music, and slip on your sheer negligee. Revel in the trappings of romance.

But if you want to love your husband with a pure, unfettered, rollicking passion, you'll need to do these three things consistently:

151

1. Daily fill that needy cup inside you with an abundance of Christ's love.

2. Pray fervently for your husband every day. (You can't stay angry at someone you uphold daily before the throne of God.)

3. Ask God to show you how to love your husband more. Scripture tells us to do all things to the glory of God. Imagine! You please God when you make passionate love to your mate. What a concept! And lest you forget the obvious, God not only invented sex, He made it fun. He wants you to enjoy it too.

A TIME FOR REFLECTION

1. Have you gathered grievances lately toward those in your circle of love? Do you consider yourself a nitpicker? Why or why not? How have negative feelings affected your relationship with your friends or family? After reading this chapter, is there anything you would do differently?

2. Think about the atmosphere in your home. Is it positive and accepting or critical and negative? How often do you seek to affirm other family members? How often do you carry on meaningful conversations with your loved ones? In what ways could you offer more positive strokes?

3. Wives, think about your relationship with your husband. How could it be improved? What can you do today to begin loving your spouse out of an overflow of God's love?

A TIME FOR ACTION

1. The next time you experience a distressing situation, practice "running to Jesus as fast as you can."

Write in your journal your reaction to this six-step process. Was it a success? Describe how it impacted your behavior.

2. Wives, plan a special evening with your husband, complete with intimate conversation, a cozy meal, prayer, fun, and romance. Be creative, choosing a setting and atmosphere you both enjoy. Read together Ephesians 5:22–33 and discuss how each of you can more fully exemplify the ideals of these verses. Commit yourself to giving your husband an evening he'll never forget. (Or you may wish to read 1 Corinthians 13, the love chapter, or that wonderfully romantic book, Song of Solomon. Even if you don't share these passages with your husband, read and reflect on them yourself before finishing your passion journey in this book.)

3. Singles, focus on a relationship that needs nurturing. Plan a fun time together, going out to dinner or a play, sharing a good book, taking a walk, or carrying on a long phone conversation. Look for ways to build up one another. Practice listening, laughing together, and sharing one another's ups and downs.

RESPOND WITH
THE HEART, NOT
JUST THE HEAD

 It was our silver wedding anniversary, and Bill and I wanted to celebrate our twenty-five years of marriage in a special way. But since he wasn't working at the time, our finances were tight. There was nothing extra for an evening out. Still, we couldn't let the day pass without some sort of fanfare or festivity.

So we decided on dinner and a movie, even though we almost never went to movies (it had been drummed into me since childhood that movies were the devil's domain). But there was a theater near us with tickets for only a dollar, so we decided to try it.

First, we ate at an Italian restaurant, using a coupon for two dinners for the price of one. The food was lousy, and we vowed never to go back. Then we made our way to the dollar theater, hoping a nice romantic movie would compensate for our disappointing dinner. But the only movie that looked remotely acceptable was (as we would soon discover) a silly, tedious film called *The Butcher's Wife*. And, yes, it was as bad as the title.

With a bit of apprehension we entered the darkened theater and sat down in the center section. As our eyes grew accustomed to the darkness, we looked around and realized we were the only two people in the entire auditorium.

That should have told us something.

We resolved to enjoy the movie anyway, but halfway through, insult of insults, the film broke and the screen went white. We waited patiently, expecting the projectionist to fix it. Then we realized with a jolt that not only was there no one else in the theater, there was also no one in the projection booth.

Bravely, my disgruntled husband went out to the lobby, looking for someone to repair our lackluster film. After a while the celluloid was humming again—only to break again a few minutes later. Out Bill went again to find the manager. Then back he came. "They're working on it," he grumbled.

But the film broke again, and again.

Finally, as Bill and I sat alone in the silent darkness, we saw the humor in the situation and burst into laughter. We couldn't stop laughing. We were celebrating our twenty-fifth anniversary sitting in an empty theater watching a movie we didn't want to see that wouldn't run anyway. Everything that could go wrong had gone wrong.

Finally, the manager gave us some free tickets and told us to come back another time.

So much for our glorious, romantic silver anniversary.

Sometimes you just can't make magic happen. But that doesn't mean you shouldn't try.

For the first twenty-two years of our marriage, Bill and I had very little privacy. We lived in a house with a master bedroom the size of a postage stamp. Okay, a shoe box.

Or a walk-in closet. There was just enough room for one person to walk around the queen-size bed. We had no lock on the door. And our tiny bathroom had the only working shower in the house, so the entire family traipsed through our bedroom to the shower at any time of the day or night.

So when we bought our current house twelve years ago, we made sure it had a spacious master bedroom with a lock on the door and lots of privacy. The size of a studio apartment, our bedroom has a retreat area with sofa, stereo, and TV, plus a sliding door and balcony. The bath area is roomy with double sinks, a wide shower, and a large oval tub in a bay of windows. We even bought a little refrigerator for our retreat so we could stock our favorite delicacies and share some sparkling cider or exotic fruit drinks without having to run downstairs to the kitchen. We figure we could hide away in our retreat for days at a time if necessary.

When either of us wants to get away from it all and spend some private time together, we'll whisper, "Wanna rub necks?" We'll slip upstairs like furtive teenagers, lock the bedroom door, put on the stereo, turn off the lights, and cuddle up on the sofa. Then we'll give each other a back rub while gazing out at the rugged desert mountains and the ocean of stars.

After thirty-four years we're getting better at this romance business. Better at communicating. Better at ignoring the small stuff that annoys and focusing on the good stuff. We're happy, content, comfortable together. These years truly are the best.

How about you? Are these your best years?

Some things just take time. They can't be hurried. You glean insights in three decades of marriage you can't possibly know in the beginning.

But some things you can learn no matter how new your journey.

And other things you can work at, improve.

No matter what stage we're in, we can all continue to grow.

I'm still learning.

I've got a lot to learn.

COMMUNICATION IS KEY

One thing I've noticed over the years is that relationships thrive on healthy communication. Without it, they may wither and die.

Strangely, in this information age of exploding communication, of worldwide Internet links and satellite hookups and live television around the globe, our communication skills seem to be dwindling. Gone is the friendly feel of extended families, back-fence neighbors, and hometown meetings.

Ironically, with the earth's population at an all-time high, people today are lonely and alone, hungering for love, some seeking it anywhere they can find it.

I think the greatest malady of the twenty-first century will prove to be a sense of isolation and alienation from one another—and from God. We're more acquainted with our electronic equipment—our TVs, computers, VCRs, and electronic games—than with one another. We spend more time talking to strangers in chat rooms or writing our email buddies than conversing with members of our own family.

The church isn't immune. Every Sunday we see anonymous faces and share "unspoken prayer requests"—a symptom of a lack of intimate sharing even among Bible-believing Christians.

What's it like at your house? Could this be your family? Do you get so busy with the daily grind of living, working, and surviving that you often miss those rare, fleeting opportunities to encourage and validate one another?

157

When is the last time you really listened to your loved ones, looked deep into their eyes, gave them an unexpected hug or kiss, told them you loved them, expressed your pride in them, cried with them, laughed with them, and prayed for them with fervent tears?

Does that question make you squirm a little? It does me. Because I know I miss so many chances to reach out with an extra hug or smile or words of affirmation.

I admit, there are days when I run from morning until night, doing things, fixing meals, cleaning, sitting at my computer, keeping appointments, even exchanging bits of conversation with my family. And yet I never once in that day stop and look them in the eye and really connect with them on an emotional level.

My day might sound something like this: "Bill, what time will you be home tonight? Don't forget to mail those bills. Oh, and pick up some milk on the way home. Yes, the plumber called; he'll be here at noon. Heather, get up; you're running late. Tom called (or Dick, or Harry, or whoever). Heather, I said get up! Will you be home for dinner? Don't drive too fast. Did you hear me, Heather? Heather? Bill, how was the drive? That bad? Yes, dinner's ready. Do you want a salad? Ranch dressing? No, the phone's not for you; it's for Heather. You're missing the news, dear. Where's the remote control? No, Bill, all the calls were for Heather. Good night, dear. I'll be up as soon as I finish this chapter."

It startles me when I realize how easy it is to go for days at a time without ever saying anything significant to those I love. Life is so often about the trivial, the tedium of ordinary living, getting through the day, keeping to schedules, making sure our lives hum along like well-oiled machinery, everyone with a job to do, everyone in his place.

But where's the love?

How do we give our loved ones more positive strokes, verbal affirmations, and spiritual mentoring during our busy, routine days? Does it just come naturally? Are some people simply more gifted at affirming others? Or is it something we can get better at with practice?

Recently, while speaking at a women's retreat in Palm Springs, I was impressed by how quick the women were to exchange hugs and prayers. They opened the first session by inviting everyone to hug her neighbors and offer a sentence prayer for their blessing. The room came alive as over one hundred women went around embracing one another and offering up a sweet cacophony of prayers. I, too, was swept into the melee, giving and receiving hugs, whispering sentence prayers and being prayed for. And, oh, how blessed we all felt by the time we'd been hugged and prayed for over a dozen times.

And that was just the beginning. Throughout the retreat, whenever someone expressed a need, there were always several women ready to open their arms and whisper a prayer. It seemed to come as easily for them as breathing. For me, those frequent hugs and prayers were the best part of the retreat. Even though I had come to minister to them, their ministry to me was far greater. I was on a spiritual high for the entire weekend.

When I got home from the retreat, I couldn't get the example of those women out of my mind. I knew the Lord was nudging me, telling me something important, showing me a principle for my own life . . . and for yours.

What is it? A remedy for what ails us.

A Hug and a Prayer

Let's admit it. Some of us are huggers and some of us are not. You know which you are without giving it a second thought, right? Hugger. Non-hugger. You know the huggers in your group, because for the slightest reason they will bound over, gather you into their arms, and give you a bear hug to end all bear hugs.

159

Personally, I'm not a natural hugger. But I love hugs, and I'm learning to give and receive them graciously. I've always admired the huggers among us, because such spontaneous shows of emotion demonstrate that these embracing beauties are already women of passion. And we could all take a lesson from them.

So if you're not a natural hugger, start practicing today.

I've also always admired Christians who, when you share with them a need, will immediately say, "Let's pray about it." And then they offer up a prayer right there on the spot. No dillydallying for them. Their prayers are winging to heaven before you have a chance to catch your breath.

Now, don't get me wrong. I often tell people I will pray for them. And I try to keep my promise. But when I say I'll pray, I usually mean the next time I have my devotions. On-the-spot prayer has always been more daunting than my natural reticence could handle.

But there's something beautiful and intimate about sharing a need and having someone immediately whisper a prayer on your behalf.

So lately I've tried applying this "hug and a prayer" approach in my own family. When my daughter came home disheartened over a broken relationship, I gathered her in my arms and hugged her and whispered a prayer for God's comfort. Right then and there. Just a few brief words, but her reaction was immediate—and positive. She felt better—consoled and encouraged all at once.

And I felt an immediate emotional connection blossom between us. We've always been close, but this was on a spiritual level. The hug and prayer touched us both. And that's the beauty of it. It blesses both the giver and the receiver.

What makes it so special?

There's something about combining physical touch with a spoken prayer that works wonders. God planned it that way. He made the simple act of touching such a crucial part of human experience that babies actually die if they aren't touched and caressed.

And prayer . . . it's the breath of spiritual life for us as Christians: communing with God, listening to His still, small voice, and connecting with Him through His Spirit. But many of us reserve the practice of prayer for Sunday morning church or Wednesday night prayer meeting. How blessed we would be if we could make prayer as natural as breathing . . . and if we could make whispered, spoken prayers a comfortable and spontaneous part of family interactions.

Moms, remember when your children were small and you kissed their knee when they fell down and got a boo-boo? Well, a hug and a prayer is infinitely better, and it works for all ages! I'm not there yet, but I'm working at being more spontaneous with both my hugs and my prayers. And I like it!

So start making it a practice to respond to your loved ones with both a hug and a prayer. That's the consummate combination—putting prayers and hugs together as God's best remedy for what ails you. Try it. You'll be amazed. No matter what the occasion, whether your loved ones are hurt or happy, celebrating or disappointed, give them a hug and whisper a prayer with them. "Help her, Lord, in this trying situation. Thank You, Lord, for giving him this victory. Help her, Father, to see Your purpose in this."

So simple, so easy. A hug and a prayer—but what a wallop they pack.

Okay, so it's not so easy. If you're not a natural hugger and not used to on-the-spot praying, it's going to feel a tad awkward at first. But give it a try. Repeat that little phrase over and over to remind yourself: A hug and a prayer . . . a hug and a prayer.

Look for everyday opportunities to bestow those hugs and prayers on your loved ones. They may be surprised the first time you sweep them into your arms and whisper a heartfelt prayer. But soon you'll all be looking forward to those brief, priceless moments together. I'm convinced there's no better way to nurture tender intimacy than with an impromptu hug and a prayer.

Heart Communication

But when it comes to communicating in positive ways with our family, there's still more we can do. Much more.

We can learn to respond with our heart, not just our head.

Romans 12:15 admonishes, "Rejoice with those who rejoice, and weep with those who weep." *The Living Bible* puts it this way: "When others are happy, be happy with them. If they are sad, share their sorrow."

This concept is so simple and obvious; yet most of us fail to apply it in our daily lives. When your loved one is hurting, open yourself to feel his pain. Make yourself vulnerable to him, allowing yourself to experience the same grief he is feeling. It's not easy taking on the hurts of another, but the impact on your loved one will be profound as he senses your oneness with him in his sorrow. By sharing his pain, you will literally be helping him to bear his burden. When we bear one another's burdens, we reflect what Christ did for us. Isaiah 53:4 tells us, "Surely He has borne our griefs and carried our sorrows."

When my baby died, I received many words of condolence and expressions of regret, and I appreciated them deeply. But what I remember most are not the words people said but the tears they shed with me. When friends wrapped their arms around me and allowed their tears to fall with mine, I felt a healing balm. Their willingness to take my grief upon themselves buoyed my spirit and reminded me of their love. To this day, I remember the tears, and they still touch me.

Dear sister, allow yourself to feel your loved one's pain. Respond to your family's emotional needs with your own heartfelt emotions, showing how much you care by freely expressing empathy and compassion. In moments of shared hurt you will forge a bond with your loved ones that times of pleasure rarely bring. Don't miss the chance to be there on every emotional level when your loved ones need you most.

And when those in your circle of love are happy and rejoicing, enter into their merriment with an eager heart, not a grudging one. Laugh with them, rejoice with them, feel their excitement and elation.

Some of us dole out our emotions like misers counting pennies. We're afraid to show others how we feel inside. Or we keep such a tight rein on our emotions for fear of losing control. Or perhaps we're embarrassed to surrender ourselves to raw, spontaneous emotion because we don't know where it will take us. If we allow ourselves to weep, will we ever be able to stop? If we give ourselves to deep, belly-shaking laughter, will we lose ourselves completely? If the genie is uncorked, will we ever get him back inside the bottle? If others glimpse our real inner self, will we ever be able to hide again?

Perhaps because we instinctively fear facing our own emotions, we often give our loved ones contrived, surface responses. Let's look at some of these unsatisfactory reactions. I've given them names, so once you've met these unpleasant women, you'll remember them . . . and avoid them!

Ms. Logic

Ms. Critic

Ms. Complaint

Ms. Argument

Ms. Neglect

How do these hard-hearted ladies respond when a loved one is in need? Let's listen in on a conversation and see.

Let's say Johnny, your junior-high-age son, comes home from school late with his Levi's caked with dirt and his new sport shirt torn. Worst of all, he's sporting a black eye. He's obviously been in a fight, the very thing you've warned him against time and again. Here's his story: "Mom, I'm sorry. I couldn't help it. These guys from eighth grade, a bunch of stupid jerks, came over and took my Walkman. Wouldn't give it back. Just stood there laughing at me. When I tried to grab my Walkman back, they all started pounding on me. Some of the other guys got into it too. It was a big free-for-all, until the principal came out and caught us. He sent me home with a note. I'm in trouble, Mom."

So how do our various women respond?

Ms. Logic: "John Allen Smith, you know it's wrong to fight. And you know how those older boys are. They're just looking for someone to pick on. They see your Walkman, and they're going to want it. Think about the consequences, John. I refuse to feel sorry for you. When you hang out with guys like that, you're just asking for trouble. That's just the way things are, so you'd better get used to it."

Ms. Critic: "John Allen, your middle name is trouble! It follows you everywhere. You're always messing up. You had no business staying late after school in the first place. Now the principal will probably kick you out. How stupid can you be, tangling with ruffians like that. You know better. Look at you! You're just as bad as they are, fighting like an animal. You look disgusting!"

Ms. Complaint: "I'll tell you one thing, Johnny Smith, I'll never buy you new Levi's and expensive shirts again. You've wrecked those. Do you think I can ever get them clean again? What do you think I am, a household drudge? And that eye! I'll have to drive you to the doctor with that shiner! What do I look like? Your personal chauffeur? And if you think I'm going to try to smooth things over with your principal, you've got another thing coming. I'll tell you what. You're going to drive me to an early grave!"

Ms. Argument: "Don't you tell me you got beat up, John Allen. I don't want to hear it. You probably started it in the first place, you with your hot temper. Just like your dad's. Always blaming other people when it's your own fault. It's a good thing those boys did get your Walkman. Now maybe you'll settle down and do your homework without that rap noise blasting in your ears."

Ms. Neglect: "Johnny, you're a mess! Go clean yourself up and put something on that eye. I can't listen to your tale of woe now. Tell me about it tonight. Right now I'm late for my appointment with my hairdresser. If I'm not there by four, she'll take someone else. Wait till your dad gets home. You're going to have to answer to him about this, you hear? Where are my keys? Have you seen my keys?"

Now that we've heard from our loathsome ladies, what is the proper response to our little Johnny's doleful dilemma? Responding from the heart with loving concern and compassion, we give our son an embrace, if he'll let us. If not, we make a point to touch him, either a soothing hand on his forehead, a gentle palm on his cheek, or a squeeze of the shoulder. Somehow we make a physical connection with him, and we look him in the eye and say, "Honey, I'm so sorry you were hurt. And I'm sorry about your Walkman. I know how much it meant to you. I hate to see your good clothes ruined, but they're only clothes. They can be replaced, but you can't. While I get something for your eye, sit down and tell me what happened. If we have to talk with the principal about this, your dad and I will be there for you. No matter what happens, you know how much we love you. We'll get through this together."

Which type of response is going to weave close emotional bonds in your family? The answer is obvious on paper but not always so apparent in real life. The next time someone in your circle of love comes to you with a need, think carefully about which response you're going to give. Remember that answering your loved one's needs with logic, criticism, complaints, arguments, or neglect won't minister to his hurts. Such responses will only widen the emotional chasm between you. Only heart responses swathed in compassion and understanding will satisfy the deep emotional hunger of those you love.

A Time for Reflection

1. Think about the kind of communication practiced in your family or circle of friends. Which technique is most often used? Is there room for improvement? Write in your journal ways you might have responded to friends or family members in recent situations. Resolve in days to come to be sensitive to opportunities to "rejoice with those who rejoice, and weep with those who weep."

2. Reflect on your family's daily schedule. Is it filled with fragments of "deadwood" conversation, such as, "Don't forget the milk. Where's the remote control? Have a good day. See you later"? Do you see opportunities you might have missed for communicating on a deeper level with the important people in your life? If your busy schedule affords no time for meaningful sharing, what activities could you eliminate to allow more time?

A Time for Action

1. Make it a point to give at least one friend or family member a hug and a prayer today. Write about the experience in your journal. Did it come easy for

you? How did your reaching out with a hug and a prayer impact your loved one?

2. Read over the following reactions. Each one reflects one of the types of responses we have discussed: logic, criticism, complaints, arguments, neglect, or heart response. Mark those responses that come from the heart. Prayerfully invite God to show you new ways to respond from the heart to your loved ones.

_____ "Don't get so upset. That's just the way life is."

_____ "What's wrong with your head? You never remember what I tell you."

_____ "I can see you're hurting, dear. It makes me hurt too."

_____ "Help me understand how you feel, so I can make it right."

_____ "Who was your slave last year at this time?"

_____ "Don't be so sensitive. Lighten up!"

_____ "How could you embarrass me like that? You might think about my feelings once in a while."

_____ "I'm committed to you, sweetheart, no matter what happens."

_____ "I don't want to discuss it. Just leave me alone."

_____ "I'm sorry I hurt you. I was wrong. Will you forgive me?"

_____ "Give me a break! I don't have time to talk about it now."

_____ "You're so lazy. No wonder you don't have a job."

_____ "It makes me sad to see you so upset."

_____ "When are you going to grow up and take responsibility for yourself?"

_____ "What you did was wrong, but I'll stand by you. You can count on me."

167

PRACTICE SPEAKING
THE TRUTH IN LOVE

 Some time after I started traveling away from home for speaking engagements, my husband made a momentous discovery. If he wanted clean clothes while I was away, he would have to wash them himself. That meant learning to use the washer and dryer.

Being the detailed, engineer-type person he is, he entered into his new endeavor with unswerving fervor. He went throughout the house gathering all the whites and all the darks. And there were plenty of dark clothes, because our daughter Kim was living at home at the time and in her "black phase," wearing nothing but black.

Then Bill marched to the laundry room and stuffed all the lights and darks into the washing machine together (I guess I had neglected to explain about sorting the clothes into color groups). He poured in the laundry detergent, and being the meticulous, detailed person he is, he poured in a cup of . . . BLEACH!

To this day we remember that event as the time our daughter went from her black phase to her tie-dyed phase! In fact, for many months we all wore tie-dye!

You might wonder how I reacted to that hapless little incident. Did I blow my top? Shrug it off? Thank Bill anyway for his effort? I honestly don't remember. I think I discovered his laundry mishap gradually, as I came upon items of clothing that were once white and were now, well, less than white. I do know that it became one of the family legends we laugh about. And it makes a great story for audiences of women who can identify with hubbies helping out, not always successfully.

Being part of a family automatically means we encounter our share of annoyances, irritations, and aggravations. How we handle them and the way we communicate with one another will determine the atmosphere in our home. Do we live in a Placid Palace (mostly pleasant and easygoing), an Armed Camp (coldly silent and on guard), or an Outburst Hotel (filled with endless shouting)?

BROODERS AND BLASTERS

The mood in our home will be largely determined by the types of communicators we are. All of us tend to fall into one of two types. We're either brooders or blasters. When we are wronged, we either sulk or rage. We bury our feelings or shoot them off like cannonballs. We suppress our needs or fling them like darts.

You know which you are. Without giving it a second thought, you know. Just as you know what your mate is, and your children, and your friends. It's basic. It's the way you're wired, how your personality is programmed. Your way of reacting to others is tied into whether you're an introvert at heart or an extrovert.

I'm a brooder. Bill's a blaster.

169

When I feel hurt, I withdraw into myself and sulk, maybe even pout a little. When Bill's upset, he bellows and blusters and sputters.

Which are you? A brooder? Or a blaster?

Let's look at each of these more closely. Men and women certainly vary from one another within these prototypes. In other words, a brooding man will be different from a brooding woman. And thankfully, most of us aren't as radical and flagrant as the examples that follow. I've given our various archetypes names to keep them straight in our minds, along with definitions of their behavior.

Ms. Stash and Stow: She stashes and stows all the things she's feeling, especially when she's angry or upset. If you cross her or rile her, she won't come back with a verbal attack. No, Ms. S&S will draw back inside herself like a glowering turtle and leave you guessing until next Tuesday why she's in hiding. If you really loved her, you'd know why she's sulking; at least, that's how she sees it.

When Ms. S&S recoils into herself, the whole house feels chilly. An expert with the cold shoulder, Ms. S&S can maintain her remote, unresponsive stance for hours, even days, making you sweat while she remains distressingly cucumber cool. Her silence speaks volumes; she can level you with an icy glare. Ms. S&S wields immense power from her lofty, fortified tower. Her muted scorn can prompt even the most stalwart to retreat. But just when she thinks she's winning, she's already lost the game, because hiding behind walls of one's own making is a lonely, dead-end pain.

Ms. Heave-Ho: When it comes to venting her feelings, Ms. H-H never leaves anyone guessing. She's fast on her feet, and even faster with a full-throttle comeback. She'll heave everything at you but the kitchen sink. You'd better duck when she starts spewing her venom and slinging those bitter rebuttals. If you cross her, you'll hear about it, and so will the rest of the world. Waving her rage like a banner, she can fulminate, hiss, rant, rave, spit, and sputter. Desperate to have her needs met, Ms. H-H nags, badgers, whines, heckles, and henpecks her mate, not realizing she is sabotaging the very relationship she's most afraid to lose.

Mr. Incommunicado: During courtship, Mr. INC comes across as the strong, silent type who makes the girls swoon. But after a few years of marriage, what appears to be a virtue may become a liability as Mr. INC shuts down his emotions and closes the shutter on his soul. When his wife and family try to break through his impervious exterior, they are repelled by his brusque demeanor and withering glances. A man of few words, he knows exactly how to wound with a disgruntled sigh or a well-aimed sneer. Aloof, arrogant, and unapproachable, he rules his little kingdom with silent contempt, daring anyone to glimpse the vulnerable, needy man beneath the iron veneer.

Mr. Hurly-Burly: Living with Mr. H-B is like pitching your tent in a lion's den. Hoping to let sleeping beasts lie, you spend your life tiptoeing around him, fearful that the slightest misdeed will rouse the raging lion from his lair. When he's provoked, watch out! He prowls his domain, growling, snarling, hissing, muttering, and complaining. At the slightest offense, he hurls diatribes and accusations. You'd swear he thrives on chaos and conflict. He's always ready for a tussle, a skirmish, or a tirade. Life with Mr. H-B is unpredictable from one hour to the next. You live in near exhaustion trying to second-guess him. You know somewhere inside the blustery beast is the caring man you fell in love with.

SPEAK THE TRUTH IN LOVE

Happy, satisfying, nurturing homes are not peopled with the likes of Ms. Stash and Stow, Ms. Heave-Ho, Mr. Incommunicado, or Mr. Hurly-Burly. Oh, yes, I admit we all exhibit some of their traits from time to time. We all have some of the brooder or the blaster inside us. It's in our nature to react one way or the other. And sadly, a few of us match one of these four lamentable caricatures to a tee.

The question is, How can we break away from our natural, flawed methods of communicating with one another and establish candid, caring responses instead? How can we avoid the Outburst Hotel or Armed Camp environment and make our homes into . . . okay, maybe not Placid Palaces, but at least, warm, safe, nurturing abodes?

It takes prayer and practice, but it can be done.

Scripture gives us the simple guideline in Ephesians 4:15: Speak the truth in love. The key to all successful communication is found in those five little words. They address both the brooders and the blasters among us. Let's look at that sentence, word by word.

First, *speak!* That takes care of us brooding souls who sulk and pout and withdraw rather than saying what's on our minds. We're told to speak, to reveal what's on our hearts, to admit our needs and acknowledge our hurts. How often could we resolve our conflicts with our loved ones if we simply told them what was bothering us rather than stowing our grievances in our hearts until they grow rancid?

Next, speak *the truth.* These days the truth has given way to political correctness in nearly every area of our lives. No longer can you say, "The garbage man is coming." He's the sanitation engineer! My husband says in jest that people used to call him "short." Now they say he's "vertically challenged."

Sometimes it takes a brave soul to speak the truth to others. We live in an age of euphemisms. The harshest realities are couched in rosy, deceptive language. The abortion movement takes the proverbial cake here by switching the spotlight from killing babies to the seemingly lofty cause of a woman's freedom to choose. They don't finish the sentence by saying what she has the supposed right to choose—the death of her own baby. That which is abhorrent to most people—the violent death of a helpless infant—seems less repugnant when the language focuses on such positive concepts as freedom and choice.

Because we live in an age of such deception and subterfuge, we women of passion need to practice speaking the truth in all areas of our lives. Calling sin what it is . . . sin! Championing the causes of Christ. Defending our fragile, diminishing rights as Christians in a post-Christian world.

But the place to begin speaking the truth is in our own homes, where we exert the most influence. Let us speak the truth to our husbands and children and all those in our circle of love. May they always hear the truth from our lips. May they be able to count on us to be candid, direct, genuine, honest, sincere. We who are brooders have the hardest time speaking the truth because our natural inclination is to stuff our yearnings deep inside and expect others to guess what we need. It's that old "If you loved me you'd know what I'm thinking" mentality.

You who are blasters have it easier on this score. You have the gumption to speak the truth, to let it all hang out, to write your expectations across the sky if necessary. But let's face it, sometimes you blasters can be a bit, um, abrasive in your demands. Sometimes you ruffle feathers and end up alienating family members.

So let's finish our verse. Speak the truth *in love*. Aaahhh! That's it. The wisdom of the ages in five little words: Speak the truth in love. Some of us speak the truth but not in love, in anything but love! Blasters who have no trouble speaking the truth may be shooting themselves in the foot by speaking harshly, critically, and destructively. The truth without love is hard, brittle, cutting, unkind. But when you assume a warm, caring attitude, you sandwich the

173

truth in love. The truth spoken with love is palatable and nourishing, a delicacy to be savored.

When we speak the truth in love, as Scripture admonishes, we no longer exhibit the traits of brooders or blasters. Instead, we become bridge builders, lovingly strengthening our emotional attachments with our loved ones and forming strong new connections with them as well. We build bridges of communication and closeness, of fellowship and empathy, of compassion and support. Our loved ones learn they can count on us to tell them the truth and to do so with loving concern.

How does a bridge builder sound, compared with a brooder or blaster? If we're going to change our way of communicating, we must develop an ear to hear how we sound to others. We need to sharpen our sensitivity to ways of speaking that produce positive results in our loved ones. Let's set up some sizzling situations and listen in as a brooder, blaster, and bridge builder respond. In each situation, pick the response that sounds most like how you would react. If you're not a bridge builder, what can you begin to do today to become more of a bridge builder in your home?

Situation 1. You find a positive pregnancy test in your teenage daughter's wastebasket. What do you do?

Brooder: A brooder throws the trash away and convinces herself it couldn't be her daughter's; it must belong to one of her friends. But feeling worried and betrayed, a brooder makes little insinuations and casts a suspicious eye at her daughter. She treats the girl coolly, taking her bad behavior as a personal attack on her parenting skills. But she can't bring herself to confront her troubled child. Secretly she hopes that ignoring the situation will make it go away.

Blaster: A blaster immediately confronts her daughter in her room and loses her cool, shouting, "How do you explain this, young lady? Looks to me like you're pregnant! How could you, after all the warnings and lectures I've given you about sex! Look at all I've done for you, and here you go out and act like a tramp! Well, if you think I'm going to get you out of this mess, you've got another thing coming! You made your bed; now you can lie in it!"

Bridge Builder: A bridge builder finds the right time and place to sit down with her daughter in a secure, affirming atmosphere. "Honey, we need to talk. I found a pregnancy test when I was emptying your trash today. I have to assume it's yours. I'm deeply concerned about you, sweetheart. I need to hear the truth. I hope you feel you can talk to me about it. If you're pregnant, you're going to have a lot of decisions to make. You know what you did was wrong. But God can help you make the right choices now. And I want you to know this doesn't change the way I feel about you. I'll always love you and be here for you no matter what."

Situation 2. You and your husband are at a party where he betrays a confidence and embarrasses you. You feel angry and humiliated. How do you react?

Brooder: A brooder says absolutely nothing to her husband about her feelings. Instead, she sulks and gives him the cold shoulder in bed. When he asks what's wrong, she snaps, "Nothing's wrong. Why should anything be wrong?" When he persists, growing more agitated over her behavior, she turns away from him and freezes him out with her icy demeanor. The next day she's still brooding, and her husband's still in the dark as to what he did to upset her.

Blaster: Before they even arrive home, she lays into him, reading him the riot act for his faux pas at the party. "You stupid jerk, how could you say something like that to embarrass me? Do you have any idea how humiliated I felt? I'll never be able to face my friends again,

175

thanks to your big mouth. How would you like it if I told them some of your nasty little secrets? You're out of your mind if you think I'm ever going to another party with you!"

Bridge Builder: She speaks after they've arrived home and gotten comfortable and relaxed: "Honey, I really felt bad when you told our friends about _____. That was something just between us. Maybe you didn't realize how hurt and embarrassed I'd feel. I love you and I want to believe I can confide in you and trust you. I'd appreciate it if you'd check with me the next time you want to share something private like that."

Situation 3. Your best friend invites you to a party you've been yearning to attend. You go with her, expecting to have the time of your life. But shortly after you arrive, your friend engages in conversation with a group of women who don't seem to know you exist. You wander around on your own, but you feel awkward and alone. You're angry at your friend for dumping you and wish you had just stayed home.

Brooder: She never tells her friend how she feels but silently crosses her off her list. *I'll show her,* she thinks with growing resentment. *We're through! I'll never call her again. It serves her right for being such a lousy friend.*

Blaster: A blaster reads her friend the riot act as soon as they're in the car. "How could you do this to me? You're supposed to be my best friend. Some friend you are! You left me high and dry while you traipsed around gossiping with everyone in the place. I know you were working the party just to get ahead. That's all you care about, getting in tight with the movers and the shakers. Well, if that's the kind of friend you want to be, don't bother calling me again!"

Bridge Builder: When her friend drives her home, she invites her in for coffee and waits until they've had a chance to relax before broaching the subject of her friend's behavior. Making an effort to keep any resentment or accusation out of her voice, she says, "I didn't enjoy the evening as much as I'd expected to. Your friendship means a lot to me, and I was counting on us sharing some time together. I admit I felt hurt when you spent most of your time with those women I don't know. I understand you need to take advantage of networking opportunities, so maybe next time I'd better skip the party and we could plan a separate outing for just the two of us."

Situation 4. You hear from various sources that your sister-in-law has been saying negative things about you. You're hurt because you thought you got along pretty well. What do you do?

Brooder: She internalizes the unkind remarks and lets them fester and grow; she dwells on them often and allows them to damage her own self-esteem. Whenever she sees her sister-in-law, she gives her a cold shoulder and avoids her, saying as little as possible. Her growing anger and resentment make it difficult for her to enjoy family get-togethers because all she can think about are those cruel remarks, which everyone else has probably forgotten. For the brooder, the remarks have taken on a life of their own; they have mushroomed into huge, dark proportions that negatively impact every area of her life.

Blaster: As soon as she learns of the unkind remarks, she wastes no time in phoning her sister-in-law and giving her a taste of her own medicine. She spews her invective in a torrent of blistering words. "How dare you say such things about me! Who do you think you are, you low-life tramp! You're lucky my brother even married you. I don't know what he ever saw in you. You're not welcome at my house again, and if my brother brings you to any family gatherings, I'm staying away."

177

Bridge Builder: She phones her sister-in-law and invites her to lunch. Over a pleasant meal she says, "We haven't had a chance to get to know each other the way I'd like. I think maybe there have been some misunderstandings we need to talk about. If I've done something to offend you, I'm sorry. I'd like us to be friends, so maybe we can start by clearing the air between us."

Situation 5. In spite of all your warnings, your son has run off and married a girl you don't approve of, thus dashing all your hopes and dreams for his future. What do you do?

Brooder: Vowing to have nothing to do with her new daughter-in-law, she emotionally freezes out her son as well. She'll show him! She won't phone or visit or give either of them the time of day. As far as she is concerned, her son is dead to her. She has closed the door of her heart to him forever. But the freeze job she's doing on her emotions will eventually turn her into a bitter, brittle, hollow old woman who's forgotten how to love.

Or a brooder may try another tack—trying to hold on to her son more tightly than ever before, nearly smothering him while freezing out her daughter-in-law with her frosty behavior and nippy innuendos. Her goal? To divide and conquer without ever raising her voice. But her scheme is bound to bring misery to everyone involved, herself most of all!

Blaster: The first time her son and his new wife come to visit, she's ready for them with a rabid tirade that's guaranteed to start her son's marriage off on the wrong foot. She lambastes her son with a heated verbal attack, shouting, "How could you do this to me? After all I've done for you! How could you be so selfish? You're going to be miserable. You know that, don't you? This isn't the girl for you. She doesn't deserve you. You're throwing your life away on her. Some day you're going to be sorry, but don't come crying to me. I warned you, and I'm not going to bail you out!"

Bridge Builder: She's not happy about the marriage, but she realizes what she does now will impact both their lives and hers. She invites her son and new daughter-in-law over for dinner and does all she can to make it a pleasant occasion. She welcomes the girl with a hug and tells her she hopes they can be friends. She treats her with kindness and respect. When she has a private moment with her son, she tells him, "You know this wasn't my choice for you, but if this is the girl you love, I respect your decision and accept her as one of my own. I love you, son, with all my heart, and I trust God to give me a love for her too. If you need me, I'm here for you. You have my prayers and support."

BE A BRIDGE BUILDER

What is the mix of brooders, blasters, and bridge builders in your family?

Yours may be a family entirely of blasters so that every get-together is a dreaded free-for-all. You know when you get so-and-so together with so-and-so, there's going to be fireworks. Everyone knows old issues and wounds will be dredged up and replayed, and the atmosphere will be charged with the electricity of bristling emotions and clashing wills. You may even avoid such gatherings because you don't want to be put through the emotional wringer again.

Or maybe yours is a family filled with brooders. In your house the reunions are anything but noisy. Relatives who haven't seen one another in years get together, exchange a few superficial pleasantries, and leave again, thinking they've done their family duty. In a family of brooders there are just as many issues and old wounds as in the family of blasters. But you'll never hear the brooders talk about

179

them, except perhaps in private conversations with one or two other family members. The air is never cleared in this brood. Age-old gripes and grievances pile up mountain high and are never brought to light. You'll hear about them only in the furtive, whispered conversations of a few brave brooders. But the old antagonisms still linger because when a family of brooders get together, you can get frostbite from the glacial chill.

Chances are your family is a mixture of brooders and blasters. During holidays and family celebrations, you can easily tell them apart, because the blasters are rehashing old ills, recounting family legends, and verbally sparring with their fellow blasters. Their boisterous, blustering, high-energy behavior rankles the standoffish brooders among them.

While the blasters bellow, the brooders sit stoically by, seasoned experts at observing and listening. The brooders have as many needs and hurts festering inside them as the blasters, so many, in fact, that they have become skilled at sorting, categorizing, and stashing their peeves and complaints on mental computer chips in their brains. At will, they can take out any particular gripe and replay it, word for word, summoning the same intense emotional pain they experienced the day the hurt was inflicted. The rest of the family has no idea of this vast reserve of grievances catalogued in the brooder's brain. All they know is that the brooder is hard to get to know, keeps to herself, and has a cold, critical spirit that keeps others from warming up to her.

Oh, if only our families of brooders and blasters could learn to be bridge builders! If only the brooders among us could summon the courage to speak up and share the deep needs of their hearts. If only they could expose their grudges and animosities to the fresh air and let them go. If only they could reach out to their families and be lovingly candid and straightforward.

If only the blasters among us could learn to be silent at times and listen and observe and focus more on the needs of others. If only they could learn to express their desires and reveal their hurts in ways that would build bridges of understanding and communication within the family.

You may be thinking, *It'll never happen. Never in a million years. I know my family, and there's no way to change them. We're stuck with what we've got.*

You may be right. There may be no way to change your family. Behavior patterns are deeply ingrained, and the ways we relate to one another are instinctive and deeply rooted in our family histories.

But there is something you can do. You can be a bridge builder, quietly building connections of love and sharing within your own family. Give the blasters in your family an extra helping of loving attention the next time you're with them. That's what they're craving anyway—attention. So let them know you're there for them. Give them the strokes they need. Focus on their positive traits and give them sincere praise. They still may be blusterers, but you will have won their heart.

And take time to seek out and affirm the brooders in your family. They have so much smoldering inside them that needs to be vented in positive ways. Encourage them to sit and talk and share their hearts. It'll take some tender loving care and gentle probing. You'll first have to win their trust. But often the brooders are just waiting for someone to notice them and draw them out. They want to share, but they don't know how.

Keep in mind, too, this advice that marriage counselors often give, especially for the brooders among us: If someone hurts you, say so. Immediately. Right when it happens. Clear the air. Get it out in the open. Don't stuff it or stew. The longer it takes for you to confront the offense, the more distant your relationship will grow.

181

Even if you suppress your pain, you can be sure the infraction will erupt some other way and weaken the bond between you.

Of course, life isn't as cut and dried as our various scenarios might suggest. The dynamics in every family are different and filled with incredible subtleties and nuances. Real life is messy and complicated and unpredictable, and real people are a mass of contradictions and cannot be pigeonholed. But I hope that by examining these basic character types and some simple principles of communication, you've gained insights into ways you can better relate to those in your circle of love. When in doubt as to how to respond, remember the scriptural exhortation: *Speak the truth in love!*

 *A Time for Reflection*

1. Think about the dynamics in your family. What is the mix of brooders, blasters, and bridge builders? Are you Ms. Stash and Stow or Ms. Heave-Ho? Is your husband Mr. Hurly-Burly or Mr. Incommunicado? How do your different personality types impact the atmosphere in your home? How do your personality types affect your children? Can you think of ways you can encourage more bridge building in your family?

2. Does a particular relationship come to mind that needs your special attention? What can you begin doing today to mend fences and build bridges of communication?

 *A Time for Action*

1. Describe in your journal the unique communication system in your family. Write down a plan of

action for increasing understanding and empathy among family members, starting with yourself.

2. Do one thing today to build a bridge of understanding between yourself and another person. Do one thing tomorrow, and one thing the next day, and so on, and so on.

12
IMMERSE YOURSELF
IN ANOTHER'S WORLD

 Growing up, I lived in a private world of my own. Feeling isolated from my peers, I created my own whimsical orb where anything and everything could happen. The landscape of my imagination was lush with stories and dreams, peopled with make-believe characters and cartoon drawings, and resounded with tales of danger, valor, and adventure. I drew my own comic books, put on neighborhood puppet shows (only because I could hide behind the stage), acted out my own dramas with a few select friends, and designed detailed floor plans for an entire town of plastic Disney figures. I named the town Pampas Valley. Using the cardboard liners from my father's dry-cleaned shirts, I created houses, shops, schools, banks, churches, grocery stores, even parks and county fairgrounds for my tiny townspeople. Spread around the floor, my cardboard town took up an entire room. More important, it stretched the boundaries of my imagination and made me believe I could actually create the astonishing worlds of my dreams.

As a teenager I drew countless sketches of horses, Disney cartoons, and portraits of my heartthrob, teen idol Ricky Nelson. I wrote short stories and poems and eventually an entire novel (a cross between Nancy Drew and Grace Livingston Hill) titled *The Clue of the Crimson Cross*. (It's still buried somewhere in a dresser drawer.) I was never bored, for I was constantly exploring the mysterious, unexplored world of my own imagination. Even at that young age I felt like a survivor. I had survived the taunts of childhood classmates and the ravages of sleeping sickness. Like the hapless scarecrow of Oz, I knew how close I had come to growing up without a brain.

But I was living a strange contradiction. Outwardly I was quiet, cautious, ordinary, and—dare I say it?—boring. I was mousy and timid, afraid to speak up or share myself or my ideas. I was a creative, impassioned dreamer trapped inside a profoundly shy, plain girl's body. More than anything, I wanted people to discover the person I was inside. I wanted them to catch a glimpse of all the marvelous, exciting things I could see through the eye of my imagination. It was as if I carried a wonderful secret I had no idea how to divulge.

Perhaps because of those aching, bittersweet early years, I've made it one of the driving forces of my life to share with others the fanciful visions and inventions of my imagination. As a writer of fiction, I've been able to do just that through my novels and stories and poems. But I have never lost that urgent, unrelenting yearning to share my inner world with others, especially those in my circle of love.

And I've often wondered if others feel that way too, if they hunger to share their inner world with their loved ones and yet never have the chance because no one comes knocking on their door, wanting in.

185

How about you? Do you have an inner world you're waiting to share with someone who truly desires to know the secret you? I suspect many of us crave the chance to open ourselves at a deeper and more meaningful level to our families and loved ones. But we haven't, because no one has asked; no one has chosen to look deeply into our souls.

Does that sound like wishful thinking or prepubescent longing? If it is, then I admit I'm guilty. As a middle-aged woman, I still feel that way, still thrive on those rare moments when I can let the dreamer loose and express my heart to someone who cares.

What baffles me is how seldom any of us get the opportunity to do just that, even within our own families. How many of us carry our dreams in our pockets like cherished family photos, and nobody ever asks to see them? Why is it we aren't skilled at stepping into another's world and experiencing his or her unique vision? Why are we content to keep our distance and revolve around one another like lonely, distant planets?

I remember a young wife who told me she was afraid her husband didn't want the best she had to give—her unique personhood, her special combination of personality, talents, and skills. What if he wanted something—*someone*—entirely different? I felt her pain as she voiced her concerns. And I wonder how many of us feel exactly that way? Do we worry that the people we love most don't really need or want the unique women we know ourselves to be? And if that is our concern, isn't it possible they feel the same way? Perhaps all of us worry, to some degree, whether those we love really need and want the real us. We won't know until we begin to open our inner worlds to them and encourage them to open themselves to us.

I don't know how to tell you to do that except to be an example by opening myself to you.

One of my favorite childhood memories is of visiting my Grandmother Gift in her turn-of-the-century Victorian house in Marion, Indiana. For me that elegant old house on the hill spelled mystery, romance, and endless possibilities. But what I treasured most were the times my grandmother would ask to see my stories, drawings, and poems. I would wait with growing impatience for her to ask me about them. And then, as she admired my sketches and read my stories, my heart would fill with immeasurable joy. It were as if I had been dying of thirst and had been given a cup of water. My grandmother cared enough to enter my world and glimpse the person I was inside. And she loved me, the real me few others bothered to see.

Then she'd go to the closet and take out the old family albums, and we'd sit side by side on the couch looking at ancient, sepia-toned photos: my grandmother as a child ill with rheumatic fever; she and my grandfather newly married, and she still a teenager; her handsome older brother, a World War I soldier, who killed himself after his wife ran off with another man. In those rare, nostalgic moments, my grandmother shared her world with me, and her stories made my imagination soar.

But those times of sharing were all too infrequent. More often, family visits were taken up with fixing and serving meals and washing dishes and watching television and carrying on dreary, routine conversations about weather, gossip, and newspaper headlines. Sometimes I would sit on the sofa between my mother and grandmother and gaze around the room at my father and grandfather and brother and sister. And silently I would cry out, *Why can't we say something meaningful? Why won't you let me see who you really are? Why don't you want to know who I am too? Why are we satisfied with so little when there's the potential for so much?*

Sometimes I wonder, *Am I the only one who thinks this way? Am I the only one yearning for more?*

How can we grow up in families and spend year after year together and yet know so little about one another?

In my father's family especially, people simply didn't talk about themselves, didn't share their inmost thoughts. Even though many were artists and musicians, they were stalwart, reserved, unemotional people. Or were they like me, filled with passion on the inside but unskilled at revealing themselves to others? The writer in me was constantly searching for clues, trying to decipher who they really were, why they behaved as they did, and what their unspoken needs might be.

Why am I telling you this? Because I want you to think consciously and deliberately about yourself and your family and whether this is an area in your home that needs improvement. How sensitive are you to the unspoken needs of your mate, your children, your parents, and others in your circle of love? Is it possible there are those around you yearning to share themselves with you, but they don't know how to begin? They don't have the words or the boldness, but with a little prompting and a bit of encouragement, they would open up and blossom like a flower.

I confess that now that I'm a grandmother, I'm often guilty of behaving much as my parents and grandparents did. When my son and daughter and their families come home for a holiday get-together, I'm so busy cooking and cleaning and then collapsing from exhaustion that I rarely have time or energy to invest in getting to know them. I seldom scratch the surface of who they really are or feel the emotion coursing under their skin. Who are these people? Why don't I know them better? Why don't they know me? We talk about superficial things—the weather, the news, the price of gas, the cost of living, what we did last Sunday, what we're doing tomorrow. Useless details. Bits of trivia. Just making conversation.

And yet, there's still so much I want to know about my children and grandchildren. And about my husband too.

So, dear sister, I write this chapter for myself as well as for you, in the hopes that we can learn to recognize those incidents that offer the promise of discovery . . . those magical moments when my grandson Luke sings a song he learned in preschool or my granddaughter Lauren gives me a drawing she made just for me. At those moments I'm reminded of the excitement I felt when my grandmother praised my drawings and read my stories. And I pray that I will seize those opportunities to immerse myself in the secret worlds of my loved ones and share their joy.

ENTER ANOTHER'S WORLD

How do we make ourselves sensitive to such rare and fleeting moments with those we love? We begin by listening.

Listen

Listening is a lost art. Many of us are so busy concentrating on what we're doing, or we're thinking about what we're going to say next, that we don't listen to what others are really saying. Listen with your heart as well as your head. Your loved one may be saying one thing outwardly and mean something entirely different. How often have you heard someone say, "I'm fine. Don't worry about me," and the real message was, "I need help, but I can't bring myself to tell you. Draw me out. Don't give up on me just because I can't find the words to tell you why I hurt."

Practice listening without interrupting. Our tendency is to break in and offer answers. We want to fix things and fix them quickly. We feel obligated to solve everyone's problems. But we can't. We don't have the power or ability to solve the ills of the world. But we can listen carefully and give our loved ones time to talk, even if it means waiting through the silences for the hard words to come. We can listen without being judgmental or critical. We can

189

show unconditional love and acceptance even when we strongly disagree with what we're hearing.

Respond

Don't just respond politely but with genuine interest, excitement, and concentration. We should respond freely with our emotions, not just our heads. (Review chapter 10 to refresh your memory.)

Our tendency is to supply rote answers or halfhearted replies. People can tell we're giving them only half our attention. Practice responding to your loved ones with thoughtfulness, eagerness, and enthusiasm. Allow yourself to enter into their joy and experience their grief. You can tell when you've tapped into their passions because their voice will grow animated, a light will shine in their eyes, and they'll be off and running, spilling their very soul.

Think about your loved ones and what excites them. Let yourself feel their passion and absorb their energy. Let them see by your response that you love them and are personally involved in their lives. Let them sense that they can count on you without reservation.

Participate

Whenever possible, take an active part in what your loved one is doing. If your husband is involved in a project around the house, join him (unless he makes it clear he doesn't need your help). If your daughter is struggling with a school assignment, help her. If your son is on the high school track team, go to his meets and cheer him on. Attend reunions, office parties, parent-teacher conferences, plays, games, and recitals if your family is involved.

Make it your policy to be there for your loved ones, whenever and wherever they need you, even if it means rearranging your own schedule. You won't be sorry. You'll see the payoff when your kids become healthy, well-rounded adults. How many times have I heard people say, "My dad never went to one of my games. . . . My parents never attended my recitals. . . . My mom was too busy to notice the ribbons I won or the trophies I brought home."

Let it be said of you that you cheered your family on in every way that counts, that you were on the sidelines, in the stands, in the front row, and in the wings, whooping and applauding and lending your support.

In case you've missed the point here, let's consider some examples.

• You can enter my world by taking an interest in my writing. Ask about my latest project. Read my books. If you tell me my novel kept you up all night reading, I'll be delighted (after all, it kept me up many nights writing!). When it comes to immersing ourselves in one another's world, my writer-friend Doris Elaine Fell and I have got it mastered. We've critiqued each other's work for over twenty-five years, and from time to time we get together for marathon sessions during which we do nothing for three days but eat, sleep, and edit each other's manuscript.

• I enter my mother's world by discussing and admiring her paintings. She's terrific and amazingly versatile, with a warm, fresh style that blends touches of Monet's bright, impressionistic colors with Thomas Kinkade's homespun nostalgia. In fact, her watercolor roses grace the cover of this book. When I'm in town, I eagerly attend my mom's art shows and exhibits. Since I have a degree in art, we can talk intelligently about her work, even though I rarely paint anymore myself.

• You enter the world of your friends by being genuinely interested in what they are passionate about and allowing yourself to catch their passion, whether it's their new car, new job, or new romance. Don't just give lip service or bide your time until you can talk about your own interests. Show honest enthusiasm and excitement.

• You enter your children's worlds by faithfully attending school activities and events. (The teachers in my family tell me how few parents actually attend these important parent-teacher activities.) Go to your son's soccer game, your daughter's piano recital, their church programs. And how about actually getting down on the floor and playing with your preschooler? How long has it been since you saw the world from your child's perspective? How long since you put your dignity aside and let your imagination run wild? Since you got down on all fours and played with action figures or had a tea party with Barbie dolls? Try it. Your child will love it!

• You enter your teenager's world by listening attentively and asking nonthreatening questions that draw her out. Be lovingly available until she's ready to talk. Don't overwhelm her with advice or stories from your own past.

Here's a current example, and I do mean *current*. About midnight, as I was sitting here working on this chapter, my daughter Heather drifted in and started chatting. We migrated to the family room after a brief stop in the kitchen to microwave steaming cups of homemade potato-cheese soup. Then we curled up on the sofa and talked for over an hour about relationship issues. I did a lot of listening, a little responding, and a whole lot of empathizing.

When she hugged me good night a few minutes ago, she said, "Mom, when we talk, I always see things more clearly. You're so wise. You always help me get centered again and closer to the Lord. I love you for that."

Wow! My daughter thinks I'm wise. Talk about feedback that's worth a million dollars.

You know, I'm so thankful I have the same special relationship with my daughters that I had—and still have—with my own mother. She's the wisest woman I know and always senses just what to say (only now we communicate mainly via email, chat rooms, and long-distance phone calls). She kept me grounded and spiritually on target through my teen years, and if I can do the same now for Heather, I'll be eternally grateful to the Lord.

• Wives, you enter your husband's world when you take a sincere interest in his profession, hobbies, and pastimes. That doesn't mean you have to bury yourself in axle grease just because your husband loves to restore vintage cars. You needn't run a marathon because he loves track-and-field events. But you might learn enough about his job to be able to ask intelligent questions. If he enjoys bowling, you might consider joining the league, or watch his favorite television show with him, or jog with him occasionally.

When Bill and I were dating, I had no interest in sports of any kind, but he loved track and field and was a former record-setting runner. So I developed a fondness for track too. We attended track meets and watched track events on TV. Soon I knew what the Fosbury flop was and recognized the names of track stars and Olympic winners. I could enter into Bill's excitement when his favorite runner won the high hurdles or the hundred yard dash.

When we were first married, I immersed myself in Bill's world. I helped him with his master's thesis, sending out questionnaires, tabulating the results, and editing the final manuscript. When he had to work, I even attended a three-day oceanography conference and took copious notes on ocean hardware design to help complete his thesis.

Years later, Bill did the same for me. When I felt called to a writing-teaching-speaking ministry, Bill gave up his career as an aerospace engineer to devote himself full-time to helping me with my ministry. So completely did he enter into my vision of what God had called me to do, that he helped me form a writers' guild in our hometown. He became president; I was vice president. We put together a board of fellow writers and put on two one-day writers'

193

workshops each year for many years. The task was comparable to putting on two weddings a year. Even though Bill has no literary ambitions for himself, he became an authority on the business of writing and spent hours on the phone each week giving advice to aspiring writers. (However, two years later, he went back to his aerospace job when I couldn't support him in the style to which he wished to be accustomed . . . meaning three square meals a day and a roof over his head.)

You know when you've entered a loved one's world because you see the sheer delight in his or her eyes. Your loved one speaks with a passion and enthusiasm that springs from the core of his or her being. When my husband mentions his new yellow Mustang GT, when my son, David, discusses his Star Wars collection, when my nephew Jeff speaks of the newest cruise ships in his company's fleet, when my daughter Heather talks about her latest heartthrob, you can see the pure joy in their faces and the animation in their body language. Their excitement is contagious.

CREATE A SPECIAL WORLD

Okay, we're getting the message, right? We know how important it is to find better ways of communicating with our loved ones, of immersing ourselves in their world. But sometimes it's difficult to know how or where to begin. How do we break the ice? How do we let our loved ones know we want to share more of their lives? Let's look at some conversation starters we might try the next time we're together.

"Honey, if you had a day to do anything you liked, what would it be?"

"Dear, is there something you've always dreamed of doing and never had the chance?"

"Sweetheart, what do you feel passionate about?"

"I'd love to see your drawings (vacation photos, scrap-book, homework, stamp collection, new car, family video, where you work, where you hang out)."

"I'd love to hear your song (your speech, about your trip, about your job, about your friends, your opinion, what you remember about your childhood, how you're feeling, what you want to do with your life)."

"I'd love to go with you to church (your recital, the big game, your school play, your class picnic, your favorite restaurant, shop for that special outfit, look at new homes)."

When it comes to our husbands, it's important to immerse ourselves in their world. But it's even more cru-cial to establish a place and a routine where husband and wife can occasionally shut out the rest of civilization (in-cluding the kids, dogs, neighbors, boss, and annoying solicitors). But how do we create such a world?

Over the years Bill and I found ourselves so busy with our separate jobs and the demands of raising a family and running a household that we had little time for each other. Rarely did we find an evening to steal away for a romantic dinner date; we were more likely to take the kids to McDonald's for a quick Happy Meal.

Now that our three children are basically out of the nest (Heather still lives at home, but with work, college, and her social life, she only rarely makes an appearance), Bill and I are making time for each other. Recently, his doctor ordered him to walk five times a week for his heart. So we take a walk through our neighborhood to the Lake Club—a sprawling fenced-in area with a clubhouse, tennis courts, a man-made lake for fishing and boating, and many walk-ing trails. After a long stroll we may grab a hamburger and iced tea at the local Jack-in-the-Box or share an antipasto salad at the nearby pizza restaurant.

On pleasant evenings we sit on our balcony and enjoy a leisurely conversation as we gaze at the surrounding

195

mountains. In the solitude of a starry night we share our hopes and dreams, make plans for the future, reminisce about the past, chat about the latest happenings with the kids and grandkids, and just enjoy being together. We have created a private world of our own to enjoy for a few moments or a few hours.

What can you do today to begin creating a private world for you and your husband to enjoy from time to time? It may require a little ingenuity and juggling of schedules, but it's well worth the effort.

EMBRACE THE STRANGERS AMONG US

We've talked a lot about immersing ourselves in the inner worlds of our loved ones. But the discussion would not be complete without considering the challenge of experiencing the variety of social, ethnic, and economic landscapes that confront us in our physical world. Being a servant of Jesus Christ means being sensitive to those who are different from us, those who come from worlds we can't begin to imagine. Just as we need to be sensitive to our loved ones, we also need to expand our horizons and embrace the strangers and sojourners among us. We need to enlarge our capacity for compassion to include those on the fringes, the lost, the unlovely, the unloved.

We can't all travel to foreign lands, but we can have a passion for reaching others with Christ's love. We can support with our prayers and finances those mission organizations that act as our arm, our purse, our heart, and our voice to reach others.

Anne de Graaf, a writer friend of mine, just got back from the jungle refugee camps of Tanzania, where she was doing research for a book. She flew in bush planes and slept in a cement cell with bats, rats, and all sorts of vermin. She ministered to homeless, starving, dying, orphaned children and poured out her love on them. She said, "My life changed in those camps. I saw. I heard. My heart understands. And I'm willing. Send me. I want to help in any way I can, in any way He leads me." She came home physically ill, with fever and chills, possibly malaria, but, as she says, spiritually well. I wish I could tell you her whole story, but she's sharing it in her book, *Into the Nevernight*. Read it. It'll change you too.

If I am to be honest with you, I must admit I am not ready to go to foreign lands and be changed the way Anne was changed. I want to love others with Christ's love, but I wonder if I'm willing to pay the price. I would like to say I am, but I'm not sure. Perhaps I'll never know unless someday that door opens for me, and I step into some remote, alien world and experience it for myself.

I suspect most of you are like me. We desire to develop loving relationships with others, but mainly on our own terms. We want others to take an interest in us, go where we want to go, do what we want to do, and chat for hours on end about our favorite topics. In other words, we want them to enter our world, where we are most comfortable and at home.

But genuine love requires us to enter the world of our beloved, even if it is a strange and different place.

Christ Is the Ultimate Example

We can't talk about the emotional and spiritual impact of immersing ourselves in one another's world without acknowledging the example of our Savior. Out of a vast, incomprehensible love, He left His perfect realm to immerse Himself in a dying, sinful world. Jesus Christ is the embodiment of sacrificial love. He demonstrated ultimate compassion by entering our world and taking upon

197

Himself the form of a man and the burden and curse of our sin.

What it must have cost the Son of God to subject Himself to the manifold limitations of the human body—becoming a helpless fetus in a woman's womb, then a crying, wetting baby, a toddling child, and finally a flesh and blood man who knew hunger, thirst, weariness, loneliness, and pain. But the worst He experienced was to become sin for us, He who knew no sin, so that we might be made righteous in the eyes of our Father God.

By invading our world and becoming one of us, Christ showed His supreme love for us. We can't repay Him for what He did. But we can exemplify His love in our own lives. He entered our world, poured Himself out, and held nothing back. He was God, and He gave His all. Imagine. What a wondrous example of love.

What can we do?

Where can we begin, we who are so puny, selfish, and frail?

We can begin one step at a time, by showing our love for others in our ordinary, everyday lives. By lovingly, wholeheartedly entering their world, whether that means playing on the floor with our toddler, attending our children's school and extracurricular programs, playing games or sports with our teenagers, walking a friend through a crisis, or giving our husband our undivided attention when he speaks.

Or perhaps God wants to take us beyond our everyday world to lands and peoples we can't begin to imagine. How will we know unless we take those first, faltering steps of faith out of our comfortable world . . . toward Him?

Are we ready? Willing?

What about you?

What about me?

On wings of faith, we can only wonder what worlds await us!

 *A Time for Reflection*

1. Think about the inner worlds of those you love. Can you describe their worlds? Do you know what stirs the passions of each member of your family? What can you do today to become better acquainted with each one? Entreat God for guidance.

2. Write in your journal, describing your own inner world. Describe your husband's world, your children's, or your friends'. How are they similar? How are they different? What has this exercise revealed that you didn't realize before?

 *A Time for Action*

1. Practice listening and responding more often to friends and family members, as well as participating more fully in their lives. For one week, keep a log of the times you listened, responded, and participated in each one's life. Note whether you've spent insufficient time with a loved one and make amends.

2. Make a list of ways you can immerse yourself in the lives of those in your circle of love. (For example, "I will attend Johnny's ball game. I will go jogging with my husband. I will help Mark paint his tree house. I will take Anna to breakfast for a heart-to-heart talk.")

3. Singles, you have a unique opportunity to impact the lives of both your single and married friends. Look for ways to be supportive, to be a sounding board, to lend a listening ear or a helping hand. Because you are not tied down to the daily demands of a husband and children, you may have opportunities to reach out beyond your borders to touch the lives of others in a special way. My single writer-friend, Doris Elaine Fell, visits the elderly in nursing homes, mentors a

199

college student in her church, and carries on a ministry of prayer and encouragement to many email friends. She recently spent many days at the hospital when longtime friends—a husband and wife—were hospitalized at the same time. And Doris has always been there for me for nearly thirty years! I can't imagine my world without her.

WHEN THOSE YOU LOVE
DON'T LOVE YOU BACK

 I never knew for sure my daddy loved me. My mother said he did. She said my dad just had a hard time showing it, but the love was there. I believed it with my head, tried to anyway, because surely my mother must know. If she said it was true, it must be so.

But in my heart I couldn't believe it, couldn't feel it. Inside I was always longing for my daddy's love. I grasped greedily for any crumb he threw me, and there weren't many. The crumbs were always couched in criticisms, in stern looks that darkened his handsome face, looks that could wither any child's spirit, looks that said you aren't measuring up, you aren't what you should be, you don't please me, I find no pleasure in you. Those were the looks and the feelings I carried with me always. I could never be the person my dad expected me to be. I was too plain, too awkward, too tongue-tied, too untalented for him to take any pleasure in me. He never said those words, but I felt them every time I was around him.

Until the end of his life, if the two of us were alone together in a room, I felt a painful self-consciousness. I would rack my brain trying to think of something acceptable to say. No matter what I said, it came out trite, stupid, inane. I, who have written over forty books and spoken to audiences large and small across the country, could not put together a coherent sentence in front of my dad.

Regardless of how daunting the task, I spent my life trying to impress my father. I hoped each book I published might somehow stir his admiration, might make him look at me in a different way, a new light. But he never read the books. He rarely even spoke of them, surely never to offer a compliment or a word of praise.

Once I showed him a videotape of my lecture series on writing, silently hoping he would see me suddenly as a daughter to be proud of. (My mother told me over and over through the years how proud my father was of me. But why did I never feel his pride? Why did he never say the words to me so that I could experience them for myself?) When the videotape was done, I waited in excruciating anticipation for my father's reaction. What did he think of the person I had become, I, the painfully shy child who had become a teacher of writing? Was he at last impressed with my accomplishment? His only remark: "Did you notice, Carole, how you kept using the same word, *exactly*, over and over?" It was his only comment. He hadn't seen the accomplishment; he had seen only the flaw.

My father, like me, was a perfectionist all his life. He was an extremely talented man, a jazz musician playing saxophone and clarinet during the Big Band era of the '40s. My mother spoke often of their courtship. Theirs was a tender, heartwarming romance straight out of an old Bogart movie. My father had the looks and rich, smooth-as-butter singing voice of a Frank Sinatra. He even had his name in lights on a theater marquee. According to family legend, he turned down a position in Lawrence Welk's band because he felt Welk's music wasn't "pure enough" and that the bandleader wasn't going anywhere professionally. Oh, well. At times we all make major misjudgments, don't we?

But my father would not attempt anything unless he felt he could do it to perfection. Many projects in his life remained undone, untried, many dreams unfulfilled. After his early days of traveling with the big bands, he rarely sang again, although he continued playing saxophone and clarinet with local jazz bands until a few years before his death.

My father carried within him an immense burden of personal pain. I know of it, not because he ever spoke of it or in any way shared it with me; I know only because my mother told me so and because I saw the effect of it in his life and his relationships with his family. He was the only child of working parents in a day when mothers rarely worked; somehow he must have felt he never measured up or must have missed out on the attention he needed, for he was driven and perhaps haunted by his own inferiority complex. He once told my mother he felt guilty for everything bad that ever happened in the world, even for events over which he had no control and for which he was obviously not to blame.

Often over the years my mother and I speculated about the events that shadowed my father's life, making him feel unwanted, guilt-ridden, isolated from those who loved him. As a child, he witnessed the hanging of a black man by a lynch mob in his small Indiana town. That event surely impacted his life and his thinking. He would not tolerate any prejudicial remarks or lack of tolerance in his children. He never mentioned the lynching to us, but my grandmother described the event to my mother, and

Keep Passion Alive on the Home Front

after my father died, we found the yellowed newspaper clipping tucked away in his private possessions.

My father's life was a series of questions for us, his family. What did he think? How did he feel? Why couldn't he share himself with us? Around his musician friends or when performing for an audience, he was outgoing, congenial, and utterly charming. What had happened to make him the silent, withdrawn man he had become around his wife and children? Had we done something wrong? Had our faith in Christ alienated this man who rarely went to church? Was it his drinking and smoking that distanced him from his family? Would he ever open his heart to us . . . or to God?

From the time I accepted Christ as my personal Savior at age twelve, I joined my mother in praying for my father's salvation. For over forty years we prayed, with no apparent results. My mother witnessed to him at times and strategically turned on Billy Graham and other religious programs when he was within earshot. Most important, she loved him deeply and unconditionally throughout their fifty-seven years of marriage. And she never doubted his love for her. But Daddy would never discuss his personal beliefs. Whenever anyone asked him a question about his feelings or opinions on any subject, his typical response was, "I don't know" or "I don't care."

Several years ago my father's health began to fail. He was in and out of the hospital with congestive heart failure, diabetes, emphysema, and a host of other problems. Still, my father refused to talk about anything that really mattered. As if talking to a stranger, I found myself able to converse with him about little more than the weather. It was the only safe, nonthreatening topic I knew. Any other area of conversation opened the door to painful criticism. No matter how innocent my comments might be, my father made me feel that I had said something foolish. One condescending glance from him and I felt miserably rejected. More than anything I feared my father's rejection. Better not to speak or reach out than to do so and feel the harsh sting of his rebuke.

When I realized my dad might die without the Lord and without the promise of heaven, however, I knew I had to do something. I couldn't talk to him. My mouth grew dry and my heart pounded whenever I made a stab at ordinary conversation.

But one day God showed me the obvious answer to my dilemma, a way to reach my dad without speaking, without confrontation, without the risk of humiliation. I would write him a letter. The written word was my forte, my career, my calling. So one day I sat down at my computer and began pouring out my heart to my father. As I wrote, I prayed and wept, wept and prayed, and wept some more until I could hardly see the computer screen. I cried all the tears I had yearned to shed in my father's arms. I cried for all the emotions and needs we had never been able to share with each other, because we were both such private, wounded people. I told him how much I loved him and God loved him. I asked him to forgive me if I had done anything to hurt him. I entreated him to accept Christ as his Savior. And I told him he never had to mention or acknowledge my letter unless he wished to.

He never did. Never mentioned it. Not once. I knew he received it because my mother was with him when it arrived in the mail, and she saw him open it and read it. Afterward he handed it to her without a word. She read it and said, "Wasn't that a nice letter?" He nodded but never uttered a sound.

One day a few months later my mother summoned the courage to ask my dad if he had ever accepted the Lord into his heart. To her amazement, he said yes. When she asked him when, he replied, "A few months ago." That would have been about the time he read my letter. Within days

205

of my letter arriving, my sister Susan visited and also spoke to him from her heart about the Lord.

The following year my father's health steadily deteriorated. He was hospitalized for three months and endured open-heart surgery and numerous painful medical procedures in the slim hope of salvaging his life. Just when at last it appeared he might be able to go home, he lost his valiant fight to a virulent, extremely contagious pneumonia. During our last days with him we were forced to wear sterile gowns and uncomfortable face masks. We weren't allowed to touch him, hug him, or kiss him. The isolation he was forced to endure and the distance we had to keep from him struck us as a tragic, ironic metaphor of our baffling lifelong relationship with him.

And yet miracles winged their way like fragile doves through those hard, despairing days. My mother's pastor, David Brooks, became my father's lifeline. My father, who had rarely attended church, now had his own personal minister who came and sat by his bed and listened to him, encouraged him, and prayed with him. In a way only God could have orchestrated, they became buddies, cronies, confidants, friends. When they prayed together, my dad sometimes gripped Pastor David's hand so hard it hurt. Through Pastor Brooks we learned of my father's budding spiritual growth, and we were assured of his salvation and commitment to Christ.

When doctors told our family there was only a 50 percent chance my father would survive the open-heart surgery, my mother, brother, sister, and I gathered around his bed and held hands and took turns praying aloud for him. We all, including my dad, wept freely as we prayed. It was the first time in our lives we had prayed together with my father. We expressed our love for one another, and for once my father's defenses were down. Over and over again we told him how much we loved him, and he told us he loved us too. And for the first time I began to believe it in my heart as well as my head.

Many emotional wounds began to heal during my father's dying days. Strange how, as his physical life was ebbing away, emotional connections were just beginning to be born, like fragile buds springing up out of frozen ground. Words I had never felt comfortable uttering before slipped more easily from my lips. The night before his surgery, my father asked my mother to forgive him for all the hurts he had caused her. She left his room and sobbed brokenly. It was the first time he had ever apologized to her. My father began to call my brother Steve "my buddy," a rare endearment that brought Steve to the verge of tears. It was as if God were giving us a glimpse of the closeness, the sweet intimacy, we might have shared with my father on this earth. And it was surely a foretaste and a promise of the closeness we will share with him someday in heaven.

CHRIST CAN MEET ALL YOUR NEEDS

I reveal this bittersweet story of my father because I know someone you love has wounded you in similar— or possibly very different—ways. But the result is the same. This someone impacts every day of your life, influences how you see yourself and how you relate to your world. This person is entrenched in your head, in your heart, and under your skin, and you can't get him or her out. Even as a grown, independent adult you are still listening to this person (or persons) in your thoughts. You allow his or her voice to dictate how you feel about yourself. You may even find yourself listening to that loved one's voice more than to the voice of God.

It wasn't until I developed an intimate walk with Christ that I could hear God's voice above my father's—the voice of a loving, accepting heavenly Father instead of a critical, distant earthly father. God's unconditional love and acceptance changed my life forever.

But first I had to realize there was nothing I could do to change my father. I couldn't transform him into the warm, accessible daddy I needed. I couldn't change the circumstances of our lives. But I could let God change me. I realized, as God loved and accepted me, so I had to accept my father just as he was and love him anyway. I learned I could filter my hurts and heartaches through Jesus' love by pouring out my brokenness to Him and receiving His comforting balm.

Christ met all my needs my father couldn't meet. Just as I filtered my hurts through Christ's love, so I also had to filter my resentment of my father through Christ, letting Him assuage my anger and transform it into His loving forgiveness. It was as if Christ stood between my father and me, my compassionate Jesus healing my hurts, diffusing my anger, so that I could love my father with godly love.

When God poured out His love on me—on His timid, fainthearted child—He gave me so much more than I ever could have asked for or imagined. God gave me the courage and strength to reach for the stars, to believe I could become a successful published author, that I could teach others how to write, and that I could stand before an audience and inspire others by transparently sharing myself. All the love and nurturing I yearned for from my dad I have received from my Father God. He has freed the passion for Him and others that was locked inside me.

And God can heal your wounds and raise His voice over the destructive voices in your mind. Whatever you are lacking, Christ can supply. He will be your mother, your father, your sister, your brother, your friend, your all in all. Jesus is the Father I always dreamed of and yearned for, the perfect Father who always knows just what I need before I ask.

But perhaps you are wondering how you can communicate the love of God to this person in your life who doesn't show you love, who constantly perplexes and dismays you. If you have tried everything you know to reach him or her—warm conversations, loving actions, selfless deeds, and lots of prayer—then you, too, might consider writing a letter and expressing your heart.

One more time I was to unfold the letter I wrote to my father; one more time I was to read the words I had poured out to him. It was a chilly, blustery October day in Jackson, Michigan, the day of my father's funeral. I was standing beside his casket, and as I read I gazed out at my mother, brother, and sister sitting in the front pew. Only my father was missing. But somehow, as I read the familiar words aloud, I sensed he was listening with a smile from the corridors of heaven.

Dearest Daddy:
I'm writing you this letter because I find I can put words on paper more easily than speaking them aloud, especially words from the heart.

I know this year has been the hardest of your life as you've struggled with such devastating illnesses. How I've wished I could say or do something to help. Perhaps all I can do is write down the words I'm too shy or tongue-tied to say face-to-face.

First of all, I love you with all my heart, more than any words can say. I feel a connection with you that goes very deep; I think in many ways we are very much alike—both very private people inside. I have always felt a deep desire to know you better—to know what you're thinking and feeling. And yet I have never known how to begin, how to reach out to you and share my heart and know yours in return. And so—because rejection would be the hardest thing of all to bear—I haven't reached out at all, except in superficial ways that felt safe.

209

Perhaps, because we kids seem closer to Mother, you assume you haven't had as much influence on our lives. Believe me, that isn't true. In conversations I've had with Steve and Susi, we've realized we have all tried our hardest to excel in our separate fields in large part to please you and make you proud of us. You have no idea how much your approval means to us or what a significant presence you continue to be in our lives.

I've reached a place in my life (middle-age, I guess), where I look back on my life and on our family, and I wish I had done some things differently. I wish when I was growing up I'd taken more interest in your music and gotten to know you as a musician and a singer. I wish I'd heard you play in the orchestra more often (I think I've heard you only a couple of times). Mother has spoken so often of your wonderful and extraordinary talent. I regret not experiencing that very important part of your life.

I also wonder, Daddy, if you felt left out when we went off to church without you every Sunday. Did we, without meaning to, make you feel emotionally distanced from us? I can only try to guess how you might have felt. I wouldn't change my growing up in the church, but if we somehow made you feel shut out of our lives, I regret that, and if such is the case, I ask you to forgive me.

I know you realize the important role faith has played in our family. But I can't help thinking that after all these years we've somehow failed to communicate the truth of our faith to you, for surely if you knew what the God we love is like, you would want to embrace Him too. And you would know that He already embraces you with an all-encompassing love.

Daddy, let me tell you about the God I know—the God who has seen me through countless heartaches and trials and even the death of my child. He is the Great Comforter, the only One who can truly understand our deepest needs and sorrows. He loves us so much there is nothing He can't forgive. He knows none of us can ever be good enough to deserve His love; that's why He gave Jesus to pay the price for our sins. He paid for mine; He paid for yours. All He asks in return is that we open our hearts and accept Him as our Savior.

Maybe you've already done this sometime in the quietness of your heart. Maybe you already know Him and just haven't said anything. Or maybe you're still wondering if God will accept you. He will. He has. He does! Unconditionally. Just as you are at this very moment in time. He loves you, Daddy. Please know that. You are loved; you are so loved! And I feel that God wants me to tell you so. He wants me to tell you He will be with you through all the hard times; He will never leave you or forsake you. Just ask Him.

My prayer for you, Daddy, is that you would experience the joy that Christ can give and the peace that goes beyond our human understanding. If you have never known that peace, He's waiting, His arms open wide. Please accept His love. It's yours for the asking.

Daddy, you don't have to answer this letter; you don't even have to acknowledge it unless you want to. I just wanted you to know what's on my heart, because you are one of the most important people in my life, and I love you deeply.

Your daughter,
Carole

 A Time for Reflection

1. What person (or persons) in your life makes you feel unloved or inadequate?
2. How has this person affected the way you see yourself? The way you behave? The way you look at others? The way you look at God?
3. Search your heart to determine if there is any action you can take to mend this relationship. Make these actions a matter of daily prayer, asking God to provide the opportunities and give you the courage to act.

 A TIME FOR ACTION

1. If you have a thorny relationship with someone you love, pray for God's guidance and intercession. Look for opportunities to express Christ's love, focusing on what you can give rather than what you receive. If you are unable to speak your heart to this person, write a letter, speaking the truth . . . in love. In other words, don't rehash old wounds or make accusations; rather, ask for forgiveness if you have inflicted any hurts. Write with compassion, honesty, transparency, and tears.

2. If you have never been able to witness about your faith to a loved one, write a letter expressing your heart and urging him or her to consider the claims of Christ. Focus on God's unconditional love and acceptance; let the Holy Spirit bring conviction of sins.

3. If you have unresolved feelings for someone who has died, write a letter to that person expressing all the things you were never able to say while he or she was alive. Then read the letter at the grave site or seal it in an envelope and tuck it away in your personal possessions for review as necessary.

PART THREE

Unleash Your Passion

for Christ

A WOMAN OF PASSION IS
PASSIONATE ABOUT HER SAVIOR

Jesus: The Ultimate
Object of Our Passion

I am weeping as I write this. Often our passion journey brings tears.

My niece Karen, only forty-two, just died after a brief but valiant fight with cancer. Bill and I and her brother Jeff were with her during her last hour as her breathing grew shallow and then stopped. We sat by her bedside in the living room of her little house and held her hands and rubbed her feet and stroked her cooling cheek. I whispered over and over, "I love you, Karen. Jesus loves you too. He's holding you in His arms."

On the stereo in the background Elvis was singing, "Farther along, we'll know all about it. . . . Farther along, we'll understand why. . . ."

And then, even as I whispered, "Karen, do you feel His arms around you?" she truly was in Jesus' arms.

Karen fought a difficult battle in many ways. Raised in the church, as an adult she wanted nothing to do with church. Her many wrong choices brought pain and heartache to those who loved her most, especially to her son and three daughters. For six years she was alienated from her own mother.

Six months ago Karen had a hysterectomy, followed a few months later by a mastectomy that revealed adenocarcinoma, an aggressive, fast-growing cancer, in the breast and eighteen lymph nodes. A few weeks later a brain scan showed three cancerous tumors on the left side of her brain. Two weeks later doctors told her the cancer had invaded her liver and lungs. She had two to four months to live.

During those months Karen refused to give up hope. She underwent chemotherapy and radiation and remained positive and optimistic, even though she lost her hair, her face grew bloated from the medication, and her body grew increasingly weak.

Through it all her spirit soared. She returned to church for the first time in years and renewed her walk with Christ. She mended broken relationships and made peace with those she had wounded, including her mother. She said, "Mom, it's hard to believe, but I am happier right now than I have been for most of my adult life."

Karen was so sure she would beat the cancer that she convinced all of us in her family as well. She was always smiling, always had a lilt in her voice, and was eager to embrace life to the fullest. Just two weeks before her death, even though she needed help getting around, she took her family to Disneyland and went on all the rides. Ten days ago when the hospice nurse came to visit, Karen sent her packing, saying, "I'm not ready for you. I'm not going to die. I'm going to beat this!"

This past week Karen could hardly walk, but she made sure she was in church on Sunday morning and Wednesday night.

By Saturday she was gone. Home with Jesus.

At her funeral, which will take place in two days, her family will share with others her formidable journey of redemption and faith. Already one woman who has heard Karen's story has invited Christ to be her Savior.

As I write these words I am still raw and weary, reeling physically and emotionally over the events of these past two days, still grieving and yet marveling over the way God works. In her last days Karen had become a woman of passion for Jesus!

Even as I'm rocked by Karen's death, I receive an email from a dear friend who tells me her husband has a deadly form of brain cancer. She said she gets up in the middle of the night and sits in the darkness and listens to the heartbeat of God. She wants God's will more than she wants life itself.

And I think of you, dear friend, as we make our way on our passion journey. I wonder what heartaches and disappointments grip you at this moment. What hard road have you traveled? What deep griefs have wounded your spirit?

How I yearn for words to tell you what I'm feeling now. Jesus is enough.

He's everything.

It all starts and ends with Him.

Have you tasted His love?

Let Him wrap you in His arms and console you with a Father's love.

He is real. He is there. He will dry your tears and heal your hurting heart.

Have you given yourself to Him?

When God made us, He breathed into us the breath of life. When that breath left my niece, her earthly life was over. When God gives us spiritual life, He breathes into us the refreshing, regenerating breath of His Holy Spirit so that we may live forever. In an instant Christ caught Karen's spirit up to glory with Him.

My friend, without Christ's Spirit you are alone in your struggles and heartaches. When His Spirit indwells you, the great God of the universe takes up residence within your inmost self. You become His temple, the place of His abode. You're never alone again. It's a marvelous, unfathomable mystery!

Some of us get so involved in the outer trappings of Christianity—attending church and Bible studies, teaching a Sunday school class, serving on committees, singing in the choir, and a host of other worthwhile activities—that we overlook the reason for all our endeavors. Christ, the God-man. It's not enough to know all about Him; we must come to know Him personally and intimately as our Lord and Savior and most cherished Friend. All of the hustle and bustle in the world won't replace a daily, close, tender walk with Jesus.

Have you known people who exhibited all the trappings of Christianity but possessed none of Christ's love?

Matthew 20:16 tells us, "For many are called, but few are chosen." Televangelist Jack Van Impe puts a new slant on this verse. He calls it the "reverse version": "Many are cold and a few are frozen."

That could describe many people in our churches across the land. They go through the motions, but their hearts are cold and dead. They know nothing about a personal walk with Christ, nothing of His inexhaustible love. God doesn't want us to be the "Frozen Chosen."

He wants us to be women of passion . . . and He wants us to feel passionately about Him. He offers us a love affair of the heart, the soul, the spirit. If you aren't feeling an emotional connection with Christ, you're missing out on what a relationship with God was meant to be.

TWO WOMEN OF PASSION

Jesus always stirs passion in the hearts of those who know Him. It's been that way since He walked the cobbled streets of Jerusalem two thousand years ago. The

New Testament describes several women who demonstrated their love for Jesus with pure, selfless passion.

John 12:1–8 tells of Jesus' visit to Bethany and the home of his dear friends, Mary, Martha, and Lazarus. The family had recently survived the staggering events surrounding Lazarus's death. His sisters had grieved deeply for their brother. They had watched in stunned amazement as Jesus approached his grave and with a loud shout called Lazarus back from the dead. The two women had stared in disbelief and then unutterable joy as their brother shed his grave clothes and walked to them unblemished and whole. Alive! Incredibly alive.

Nothing would ever be the same for that family. They could never look at Jesus in the same way again, as a mere mortal subject to the laws of nature. He had superceded those laws, had triumphed over death to restore to them their beloved brother. He had done for them what no other person could do.

Now, with the memory of Lazarus's resurrection still fresh in their minds, the brother and sisters were spending a quiet evening with Jesus at their home. Martha was busy serving dinner as Lazarus sat relaxing at the table. But Mary couldn't sit idly by. Too many unexpressed emotions were churning in her heart. She had to show Jesus how she felt about Him. But how? What could she possibly do to reveal her deep devotion? Then she had an idea. She remembered something of great value the family had been saving for a rare and special occasion.

Verse 3 tells us, "Then Mary took a pound of very costly oil of spikenard, anointed the feet of Jesus, and wiped His feet with her hair. And the house was filled with the fragrance of the oil." Ah, what ardor Mary must have felt for her Lord.

Imagine the moment. Mary kneeling beside Jesus, taking His feet in her tapered fingers, pouring out the oil in slow, glistening drops, then sweeping up her long ebony hair and spreading the oil gently over His calloused heels and toes, rubbing His bronzed, earth-toughened feet with her silky, flowing tresses. What an act of passionate devotion.

Judas was there in the room too, and when he saw what Mary was doing, he jumped up and protested. Had Mary gone crazy, wasting precious oil on Jesus' feet? Water would cleanse the grime from the dusty roads. Why spill out expensive oil?

But Jesus answered Judas's protest with His own rebuke, saying, "Let her alone; she has kept this for the day of My burial" (v. 7). Jesus not only accepted Mary's demonstration of love, but He approved it and recognized it as a symbol of His approaching death and burial.

Another woman expressed her adoration for Jesus as He sat eating in a Pharisee's home. Notice the intensity of her feelings and observe how complete and unconditional was Christ's acceptance of her, as expressed in Luke 7:

> And behold, a woman in the city who was a sinner, when she knew that Jesus sat at the table in the Pharisee's house, brought an alabaster flask of fragrant oil, and stood at His feet behind Him weeping; and she began to wash His feet with her tears, and wiped them with the hair of her head; and she kissed His feet and anointed them with the fragrant oil.
>
> VERSES 37–38

When the Pharisee protested with much indignation that this woman was a sinner, Jesus answered:

> "Do you see this woman? I entered your house; you gave Me no water for My feet, but she has washed My feet with her tears and wiped them with the hair of her head.
> "You gave Me no kiss, but this woman has not ceased to kiss My feet since the time I came in. You did not

anoint My head with oil, but this woman has anointed My feet with fragrant oil. Therefore I say to you, her sins, which are many, are forgiven, for she loved much. But to whom little is forgiven, the same loves little."

And He said to her, "Your sins are forgiven. . . . Your faith has saved you. Go in peace."

VERSES 44–49

Can you feel what this woman must have been feeling? She had learned that Jesus would be dining at the Pharisee's house, so she slipped in uninvited. Now she stood behind Jesus, weeping. She had done so many bad things, made so many wrong choices. Because she had broken the laws of both God and men, everyone looked on her with contempt. They sneered and called her a sinner.

But not Jesus. When He turned and looked at her, there was only compassion in His eyes.

No one else had ever made her feel loved like this.

Jesus' love for her prompted a depth of response she had never experienced before. The emotion was more than she could contain. The tears came fast and hard; she couldn't hold them back. She knelt down beside Jesus and let her tears wash the dust from His feet. She wrapped her long hair around His feet and dried them. Then she bowed her head and kissed His feet with her lips. Not once or twice, but over and over, kiss after kiss. And finally she reached for the alabaster flask she had kept hidden in the folds of her flowing skirt. If the Pharisees saw it and realized what she planned to do with the precious oil, they would surely snatch it from her.

Even as her lips moved over Jesus' feet in lingering kisses, she opened the flask and poured out the fragrant oil, swabbing the cool liquid over His coarse skin. How soothing and refreshing that oil must have felt on Jesus' weary feet in the heat of the day.

221

Have you ever felt such passion . . . to kiss your beloved's feet and wipe them with your own hair?

Have you felt that kind of passion for Christ?

Jesus welcomed such passion. Read again what He said to the Pharisee. Jesus rebuked the man for demonstrating no loving concern. "You gave Me no water . . . no kiss . . . you did not anoint My head with oil."

But He praised the woman for showing her love with such passionate abandon. "She has washed My feet with her tears and wiped them with the hair of her head. . . . This woman has not ceased to kiss My feet since the time I came in. . . . This woman has anointed My feet with fragrant oil."

The message is clear: Jesus wants us to love Him with a passion that rouses our emotions and propels us to impassioned action on His behalf. He told us so Himself in the great commandment. We started our passion journey with this verse and now we come full circle back to it, the very core of our heart quest. Jesus said in Mark 12:30–31:

> *"And you shall love the Lord your God with all your heart, with all your soul, with all your mind, and with all your strength." This is the first commandment. And the second, like it, is this: "You shall love your neighbor as yourself." There is no other commandment greater than these.*

What is God asking for if not passion? Hearts ablaze with love for Him.

God desires that we love Him with every part of our being—our emotions, desires, affections; our will, our deepest center; our intellect and understanding; our physical strength, vigor, and energy.

Imagine what we would be like if we harnessed all our faculties for the sole purpose of loving God. We can't begin to comprehend what that would feel like, can we? Or what impact it would have on our lives. And what would our families be like if we loved like that? What would our world be like?

We love God with such a fractional, minuscule part of our being. Our love is so transient and shallow, so fleeting, so rooted in our own selfish desires. And yet Christ patiently holds out to us His standard of excellence. "Love Me with all your heart, soul, mind, and strength." While our love for Him is pale, meager, and flawed, His love for us is bountiful, unconditional, and sacrificial. He loved us while we were still sinners and died for us.

HOW PASSIONATE ARE YOU?

As we near the culmination of our passion journey, let's pause for a time of reflection. Think about how far we've come together. What have you learned about yourself? About your relationship with God and those you love? Do you feel you know yourself better today than when you first opened this book?

Take a moment, look inward, and ask yourself, *Who am I?*

Have you noticed your perceptions of yourself are constantly changing? One day you're up; another day you're down. One minute you feel okay; another minute you may feel worthless and unloved.

Security comes when we see ourselves through the mirror of a truthful, unchanging standard. The Bible is that mirror, reflecting who we are, not just who we *think* we are.

Scripture tells you who you are. You are a woman who was fashioned by God, your Creator, to be a unique individual with special talents and gifts. In Psalm 139:13–16, David says, "You have formed my inward parts. . . . I will praise You, for I am fearfully and wonderfully made. . . .

223

When I was made in secret . . . Your eyes saw my substance, being yet unformed. And in Your book they all were written."

You are someone who was separated from your Creator by your sinful choices. But God loves you so much that He gave the best He had, His beloved Son, to redeem you. Romans 5:8 says, "But God demonstrates His own love toward us, in that while we were still sinners, Christ died for us."

If you have confessed your sin and in faith received Jesus as your Savior, you are a new person in Christ. Second Corinthians 5:17 says, "Therefore, if anyone is in Christ, he is a new creation; old things have passed away; behold, all things have become new."

As a child of God, you are loved by the Father. His Holy Spirit lives in you and communes with you, so that you are never alone and never unloved. "Behold what manner of love the Father has bestowed on us, that we should be called children of God!" (1 John 3:1).

Dear sister, if you have never accepted Christ as your Savior, His Spirit is wooing you now. I asked you once before, but perhaps you weren't ready. So I ask again. Do you hear His voice in the silence of your own soul? Do you hear His call in the sudden pounding of your heart?

Somehow you know that all of your life has led up to this moment. Invite Him in. Ask Him to forgive your sins and be your own personal Savior. If you doubt His willingness to forgive you and make you pure again, remember that the woman who sought Jesus out at the Pharisee's home was described as a sinner. Even the Pharisee knew of her sins. But after she washed Jesus' feet with her tears, our Lord told the Pharisee, "Her sins, which are many, are forgiven, for she loved much." Then Christ turned and said to the weeping woman, "Your sins are forgiven. . . . Your faith has saved you. Go in peace."

Will you bow before Christ like this woman and weep tears of repentance? Will you express your sincere sorrow for your sins? Will you bow before Jesus and proclaim your love for Him, figuratively washing His feet with your hair? He's waiting, watching, ready to embrace you with His limitless love.

Or maybe you know Christ personally, but your relationship has grown cold and distant. Maybe you're ashamed of the way you've lived your life in recent years. You've failed God in so many ways. It has been so long since you've prayed that God seems like a stranger, distant, remote, uncaring.

My niece Karen felt that way. She had shut God out for most of her life. He had become a stranger to her. Worse than a stranger. She had forgotten Him.

But He hadn't forgotten her. He was ready to welcome her back with open arms. He forgave her, wiped the slate clean, and restored their relationship. Christ gave her a wellspring of joy and peace to sustain her through the darkest days as her physical life ebbed away.

Christ is waiting for you too, watching, yearning to shower you with His love and receive your love in return. Let His Spirit ignite His love in your heart and make you a woman of passion for Him.

 *A Time for Reflection*

1. Imagine yourself in the place of one of the women who anointed Jesus' feet with precious oil. How would you feel? What would you say to Jesus? What do you think He would say to you?
2. If it seems that Jesus has been a stranger to you, reflect on reasons for that distance between you. What can you do to close the gap in your relationship with Him? Is there any unconfessed sin

in your life that has broken your fellowship with Christ?

 *A Time for Action*

1. Since you can't personally anoint Jesus' feet with oil, what can you do to show how much you love Him? Make a list of things you can do today to express your loving devotion for Him.
2. In your journal describe your relationship with Christ as you see it today. Write freely and in detail, honestly searching your heart for the truth. Do you have a close, intimate walk with Jesus? Or has your love for Him grown cold?
3. If you have never asked Jesus to forgive your sins, do so now, inviting Him to be your Lord and Savior. Write your prayer in your journal. In the next few days, tell at least three people that you have committed your life to Christ.

    If you already know Jesus as your Savior but have strayed from His side, ask Him to forgive you and restore you to fellowship with Him. Share your good news with your family and others in the days to come.

    (As I mentioned before, I'd love to hear of your decision to accept Christ or of your renewed commitment to Him. Write me at Fleming H. Revell or email me at cgiftpag@jps.net, so that I may uphold you in prayer.)

INTIMATE ENCOUNTERS
WITH THE LOVER
OF YOUR SOUL

 I was on vacation in Florida, visiting my brother and sister and their families. My mom had flown in from Michigan, making our "family reunion" even more special. And to add to the frivolity, there were lots of aunts and uncles and cousins to visit as well. For two solid weeks we all chatted, shopped, cooked, ate, played games, reminisced, shopped some more, chatted some more, and ate a whole lot more. We had a marvelous time.

But as the days passed, amid all the merriment and festivities, I noticed something odd. I was feeling increasingly dispirited, emotionally on edge, even irritable. I should have been having fun, and on a surface level I was. But inside I was empty, needy, melancholy. *Where is this*

coming from? I wondered. *How can I be having such a wonderful time and yet still feel so unsatisfied?*

And then one day it dawned on me. Struck like a sudden revelation. My problem was that I was spiritually depleted. For two weeks I had been with other people every minute of the day and night (I even shared a room and a bed with my mom). Not once since I had arrived had I spent time alone. No time for myself. But more important, no time for God.

Don't get me wrong. My family members are Christians who truly love the Lord. During those two weeks, we talked many times about what God was doing in our lives, sharing vital lessons He was teaching us. We went to church and worshiped and prayed and listened to Christian music. We didn't do anything I felt God would disapprove of, so I wasn't suffering from guilt.

But for two weeks we were so busy "visiting" that I hadn't had my daily devotional time with Christ. Hadn't been refilling my cup in His presence. I was starving, dying of thirst, gasping for breath, slowly being asphyxiated spiritually. Without my personal daily "fill-up" of His Spirit, I was withering on the vine, drawing only from my own resources. It wasn't that I had done something wrong to sever our fellowship; I had simply starved it by neglect.

It was a powerful lesson for me, the realization that without my daily sustenance from God, I would slowly deteriorate, regress, weaken, and shrivel. I could not survive without Him. Okay, survive perhaps, but I could not thrive. I could not flourish without abiding in Him on a day-to-day basis. Perhaps even hour to hour. I could feel myself breaking down, my strength waning, my spirits sinking, my emotions growing cold, my irritations rising, a sense of malaise and hopelessness taking over. All of this happening while I was supposedly having the time of my life.

What a lesson those two weeks were for me, a dramatic reminder of my total dependence on Christ. His Spirit lives within me, but if I don't take time to fellowship with Him, I grow remote and disconnected, and I close Him out. He does not move. He is always there. But when I quench Him by ignoring Him, I smother myself as well.

That's why I want to make this chapter the apex, the high point, the climax of this book. What we are going to talk about here is the lifeblood of your walk with Christ. We are going to examine step-by-step the process of establishing a consistent, enduring fellowship with Him.

Why is this topic so important?

Because even though I know how vital my daily devotional time with Christ is to my spiritual survival, I still find myself resisting the impulse to spend time with Him. You would think I would know better, that I would make it a point never again to miss a day of communion with Him. But regrettably that's not the case. There are still days when I let other things crowd in and consume my time, days when I tell myself, *Oh, it won't hurt to skip reading your Bible for just one day. You prayed yesterday; you're okay for today.*

If I were to guess the number one problem Christians struggle with in their spiritual lives, it would be this: maintaining a consistent time of daily prayer and Bible study.

It's been a challenge for me for most of my adult life. In recent years, by the grace of God, I have discovered ways to ensure that I keep my appointments with God more often than I miss them. But it's still not easy. Even though I know Christ is my salvation, my lifeblood, my food and drink, the very air that sustains my spirit, my natural inclination is to try to go it alone, to do my own thing, to tell myself, *Time with God isn't really that necessary.*

But it is.

The more time I spend with Him, the more aware I am of the depression, discouragement, and spiritual apathy that seeps in when I allow myself to disconnect momentarily from His fellowship. It plays like clockwork: Time with Him equals love, joy, peace, contentment, optimism, emotional stability, patience, and a host of other positive qualities. Time away from Him equals gloom, hopelessness, feelings of inadequacy, aimlessness, irritability, doubt, and fear.

You can gauge whether you're spending enough time with Christ by which set of characteristics best describes you.

What a difference a day makes when you've been with your Savior. Right? I trust we agree on this one: Christ is our lifeline. So what daily habits can we practice to nurture a close relationship with Him? We need to establish daily mini-retreats with Jesus.

In this chapter we will examine twelve steps for turning our devotional lives into intimate, soul-stirring encounters with the Lover of our souls. Prayer and Bible study become mini-retreats during which we escape the clamor of everyday living and flee into the comforting presence of God, a time to re-center ourselves in Christ, reminding ourselves *who* we are and *whose* we are.

You may say, "I have no time in my life for mini-retreats. My schedule is packed from morning until night." If that's the case, then you especially need to carve out time every day for a mini-retreat with God. They are not optional; they are a necessity if we are to abide in Christ and find strength to navigate through our busy, hectic, demanding days. Every day we need to slip away from our busy routines into the presence of Jesus where we can sit at His feet, bask in His light, feel the comforting warmth of His love, and hear His still, small voice in our hearts. If we're too busy to fit in a mini-retreat with God each day, then our lives are too orchestrated, our schedules too packed with duties God never asked us to bear.

Even Jesus, the Son of God, needed to get away from the crowds and spend time alone with His Father. Scripture speaks of Jesus going off alone to pray and commune with God, often for days at a time. If even the Son of God felt the need to get away and commune with His Father, how much more do we need private time with our heavenly Father? For Jesus, those times of communion brought restoration and refreshment and equipped Him to return to His ministry with renewed vigor and strength. They will do the same for us.

A retreat suggests getting away from our usual jam-packed schedule for a time apart, separating ourselves from duties and demands, removing ourselves physically, mentally, spiritually, and emotionally, so we can regroup, relax, clear our minds, and compose ourselves. It is a time to shut out everything in our lives except God, a time to focus wholly on Him, to feed on Him and be replenished by His Spirit.

MINI-RETREATS

What exactly is involved in a mini-retreat? Following are twelve steps that will help you create your own private mini-retreat and turn your devotional time with the Lord into an experience of joy and intimate sharing.

Meet God Alone in Your Room or Home

The first step is to find your own private "world" where you can respond freely to God. Do you have a favorite alcove in your bedroom? A cozy corner on the sun porch? A favorite couch in the family room? A sunny spot in the kitchen nook? A redwood bench in your garden? A front porch swing? If you can think of no place where you can be alone, then it's time to consider setting some personal boundaries in your life and discussing with the people in your home your need for privacy.

Is there a time each day when you can be alone with God? What about after your husband and children or housemates have gone to bed or after they've gone to work and school? You early birds may want to rise a half hour earlier in the morning for your mini-retreat; you night owls may consider staying up an extra half hour. If you find yourself with an unexpected block of time when everyone is out of the house, you may want to seize the moment and expand your mini-retreat into a leisurely banquet with God, letting yourself relax in a delicious, unhurried, timeless communion with Christ.

Set the Mood or Create an Atmosphere with Soothing Music

This is your private retreat with God. Do whatever you need to do to make it special, to set the right mood. Do you love music? What kind? Classical? Traditional hymns? Praise choruses? Contemporary Christian music? Instrumentals especially provide good background music because you won't be distracted by the words. Select your favorite CDs and let them create the right ambience for your personal time with the Father. God will use music to prepare your heart to enter His presence.

Try to Remain Free of Time Restraints

If you have to watch the clock, it's difficult to feel you're communicating with the timeless God of the universe. Try to set aside at least an hour, for as you allow yourself to become immersed in your Savior, you may lose all track of time. Watch for unexpected opportunities when everyone is out of the house for an evening or when you have Saturday morning all to yourself. Those who must live by the clock will need to be especially creative in carving out special occasions for mini-retreats.

Spend the First Few Minutes Quieting Your Heart before God and Focusing on the Person of Christ

Sometimes I close my eyes and picture Jesus in physical form; sometimes I gaze out at the mountains from my bedroom and imagine a holy, majestic God in all His power and glory. Often I bow my head and wait on His ministering Spirit.

Psalm 46:10 tells us, "Be still, and know that I am God." In the absolute stillness of a heart bowed before Him, God will reveal Himself in ways we can't begin to predict or understand. Don't be afraid to be silent before God, for as you quiet yourself before Him and open yourself to Him, He can manifest Himself in ways He wouldn't otherwise.

Pray Aloud

I often keep my eyes open and speak to Christ as if He's sitting beside me, friend to friend. He is! I talk to Him in conversational style, picturing Him in the sky or imagining Him sitting across from me or holding me in His arms. Silent prayer is also fine, but during your mini-retreat, you can speak aloud to God as you would to your most beloved companion. Verbally articulating the words also forces you to organize your ideas and gives resonance to your feelings in a way that hones and clarifies your thinking.

Confess Your Sins and Receive His Forgiveness and Cleansing

Recently, while flipping idly through a plethora of television channels, I came upon a medical program that

233

caught my attention. A woman was undergoing surgery to remove a two-hundred-pound tumor that had wrapped itself around her body like a bun around a hot dog. That's right, I said two hundred pounds of appalling, unsightly tumor.

The operation was an all-day marathon with several surgeons slowly and meticulously cutting and tying off arteries and capillaries one by one. When they had finished their exhausting task, they disposed of the monstrous tumor by rolling it off the bed into a dumpster. It took three men. I wanted to look away, but I couldn't. It was too fascinating.

But what amazed me most were the before and after pictures of the patient. Before surgery she had looked enormous. The tumor had imprisoned her, incapacitated her, nearly garroted her, so that she could barely walk or function. But the real shock came after the surgery. Inside that gargantuan tumor was a tiny woman—petite, slim, with lots of vim and vigor. And now at last she was free to be the happy, fulfilled, productive person she was meant to be.

I couldn't miss the metaphor in this story. Many of us live lives of quiet desperation, going around with a two-hundred-pound tumor of sin and guilt and shame wrapped around us. We can't function the way we would like because our secret shame nearly strangles us. We operate out of a gnawing sense of guilt. We are imprisoned by sins that weigh us down, overwhelm our spirits, and choke our spiritual lives. Some of us are so bound by guilt and burdened by unconfessed sin that we can't begin to accomplish anything for Christ.

But we don't have to live that way.

First John 1:9 says, "If we confess our sins, He is faithful and just to forgive us our sins and to cleanse us from all unrighteousness." Let Christ cut away that gargantuan tumor of sin that envelopes you and free the vibrant, vigorous woman inside. The longer the amount of time you allow between your sinful deeds and confession, the greater the load of guilt you will carry. Don't let yourself become bogged down by guilty feelings. Why stagger under such a burden when Christ is willing to wipe the slate clean every day? His mercies are new every morning. Read Psalm 51 and pray with the psalmist, "Wash me, and I shall be whiter than snow. Make me to hear joy and gladness. . . . Hide Your face from my sins, and blot out all my iniquities. Create in me a clean heart, O God, and renew a steadfast spirit within me" (vv. 7–10).

Every day during your mini-retreat, confess the sins that come to mind and ask God to reveal hidden sins. Ask Him to show you the wrongs that need to be righted with others. Experience the pure joy of being guiltless before a holy God, washed, set apart, and restored by His matchless grace.

Sing to the Lord

Over and over in Scripture God urges us to sing to Him. Psalm 59:16 says, "But I will sing of Your power; yes, I will sing aloud of Your mercy in the morning." Psalm 68:4 admonishes, "Sing to God, sing praises to His name." Psalm 89:1 declares, "I will sing of the mercies of the LORD forever; with my mouth will I make known Your faithfulness to all generations." Clearly, God delights in hearing us sing His praises.

And we are blessed as well. The Lord touches our emotions through song. Singing opens our hearts so that His Spirit can minister to us. I love to sing aloud to God when only His ears can hear. I use old hymnbooks and song sheets containing choruses and praise songs, and sometimes I make up my own songs and sing them to Jesus. Singing His praises will stir your emotions and fill you with an overflow of love for your Savior.

235

Wash with the Word and Quote Scripture to God

Several years ago I was teaching at a writers' conference with Jim Russell, a successful businessman and founder of the Amy Awards, a foundation that gives generous cash awards to writers who most effectively communicate biblical truths to a secular audience.

Someone at the conference asked Jim, "To what do you attribute your amazing success?" His answer was simple and compelling: "I read the Bible every day, without fail. Without fail."

His answer convicted me, for in spite of my good intentions, my Bible reading was sporadic at best. Sometimes I managed to go for weeks without missing a day, but at other times, days would pass before I got back into the Word. After hearing Jim's quiet and sincere reply, I knew I had to find a way to read the Scriptures consistently.

One morning as I stood at the mirror washing my face, I thought, *This is it—the secret to reading the Bible every day.* Just as I maintained a daily ritual of getting up and washing without a second thought, so I would establish a daily routine of washing with the Word. It would be the first thing I did every morning, before I got swept into the demands of the day.

Now when I wake in the morning, one of my first thoughts is, *Wash with the Word.* I keep my Bible on my bedside table, so I don't even have to climb out of the covers. I grab my Bible, settle back down, and read leisurely, allowing God's Word to wash my heart and mind and set the tone for the day. I spend a few minutes in prayer and sometimes read an entry or two from Oswald Chambers's *My Utmost for His Highest* (both the original and revised editions, so I can compare the subtleties of the language). If time permits, I reach for my Word and prayer journal, a looseleaf notebook in which I write Scripture verses that especially speak to me, along with prayer requests and praises.

If you haven't already done so, I urge you to establish your own daily habit of "washing with the Word." Find a time during your day when you can make Bible reading a natural part of your routine. Secure a notebook and begin your own Word and prayer journal as well, writing down verses that minister to you in a special way. Memorize your favorite verses and repeat them back to God during your prayer time. The Bible is God revealing Himself to us in words. There is something beautiful and awe-inspiring about quoting God's Word aloud in His presence.

Use Body Language

Just as we need to engage our entire mind and emotions in our worship, so we should feel free to respond to God with our physical body. I rarely just sit and pray with head bowed and hands folded. As I converse with my Father God, I respond in a variety of ways. At the prompting of His Spirit, I may stand and open my arms wide or lift my hands to the sky or bury my face in my hands. I may recline on the sofa, or sit in my favorite rocker, or kneel on the floor with my head on a chair. Sometimes I walk from room to room, gazing out windows as I talk to God. When my heart is heavy, I may lie facedown on the floor. Some believers use sign language, mime, or even interpretive dance in their worship. Determine what feels right for you. What posture or stance makes you feel most connected with Christ? Let your body language be a natural extension of your worship.

Pray from Your Passions—and with Passion!

The purpose of this book is to help you become a woman of passion, a woman who is in touch with her emotions and expresses them freely and fully. Nowhere is that depth of passion more vital and necessary than in your private conversations with your Savior.

Given the fact that we have the privilege of entering the presence of our Creator, the almighty God of the universe, why is it that our prayer time so often seems like a burdensome duty?

Frankly, I think God is as bored with dry, dusty prayers as we are. How often do we recite our prayers as if going through our Christmas list? And how often do we fall asleep during our prayers? God may wish He were snoozing when He hears some of our tedious, monotonous petitions.

I confess, when I was in college I often found morning devotions dreary and dutiful, but I felt obligated to maintain a good example. So I was up at 5 A.M., while it was still dark, kneeling on a cold, hard linoleum floor in the cramped prayer room with others who looked just as sleepy as I was. My Bible classes required what seemed like prodigious amounts of reading, so I was always playing catch-up with my Bible studies. I often read Scripture just to complete my assignments or to prepare for a test. Needless to say, those devotional times were not spiritual benchmarks for me. Rarely during those early morning hours did I feel a strong emotional connection with the person of Christ.

Perhaps I needed the consistent discipline of those predawn devotions, but the prayer times I remember most fondly are the evenings I spent alone in my dormitory room, looking out across the darkened campus and talking aloud to the Lord, pouring out my heart. During those hours of prayer and Scripture reading, I experienced fellowship with the person of Christ. I communed heart to heart with my Father God, not merely checking off a laundry list of prayer requests or plowing through my assigned reading in Leviticus or Lamentations.

How does God want us to meet Him in that secret place of prayer? With hearts wide open and transparently vulnerable. With passionate abandon, relinquishing all we are, all we hold in our hands, and all our preconceived notions to the limitless power and potential of His Spirit.

When we enter God's presence, He wants us to speak freely from the deepest wellspring of who we are. Are we happy, sad, angry, bored, fearful, anxious, needy, discouraged? Don't be afraid to show Him your emotions. Reveal what you love, hate, and fear the most. Let your adoration for God ignite and flame in your heart until you can't possibly hold back your outpouring of devotion.

Let yourself weep. Many times I have come to the point of tears in my supplications. I have sobbed out my needs or sorrows or failures or frustrations. I have wept when I felt His cup of love overflowing within me. Few things are more healing and restorative than weeping unabashedly in the arms of God.

When is the last time you wept brokenly for what Christ suffered for you? How long since you wept for lost sinners or for a hurting world?

Be Yourself before God

Isn't it amazing that God invites us to come to Him just as we are? That He accepts us and loves us unconditionally, regardless of our past? He doesn't ask to check our credentials, our heritage, or our background. We don't have to give Him a list of accomplishments or worry that we don't measure up to His standard of holiness. Through Christ we have access to the throne of God. Our heavenly Father sees us through the filter of His Son's sinlessness. As His forgiven children, washed spotless in the blood of the Lamb, we can stand before God with nothing to hide. No shame. No guilt. We can be completely ourselves before Him. So let us luxuriate in that blessed freedom!

Approach Him just as you are. Let the masks drop. Speak your heart. Be real with God. Let Him see your brokenness, your blemishes, your rough edges. Tell Him exactly how you're feeling at the moment, even if you have to say, "I don't want to talk to You now, Lord. I don't feel close to You."

239

Even if you are anxious or hurt or angry, tell Him how you feel. Express your deepest needs. He works with our honesty. He works with whatever we give Him, so give Him everything, the good and the bad. Hold nothing back.

I was the shy, self-conscious child who often felt discomfort in the presence of others. Did they like me? Approve of me? Were they snickering behind my back? Would I ever measure up? Ever be good enough? Would they laugh if I poured out my heart? Reject me if I unveiled the real me? Would they understand the deepest hungers of my heart?

As much as I treasure the love of my family and friends, I must admit that God is the only one with whom I feel absolutely no self-consciousness. I feel more comfortable communing with Him than sharing myself with my dear family and friends. As much as I cherish those in my circle of love, I am more myself with my Father God than with any person on this earth.

How about you? Are you at ease in the presence of Christ? Can you be yourself, holding nothing back? Can you tell Him anything? Can you let Him see you without the masks, without the pretense and facades? Just you? Just as you are? Oh, the deep, luxuriant joy of being utterly ourselves in the presence of our merciful, compassionate Savior!

Surrender Yourself Afresh to God

I urge you to catch the vision of God's call on your life. There is a transcendent joy in total surrender to His will. It's that delicious sensation of lying back on the water and letting the gentle waves carry you where they will. He knows the direction, the destination, and the best way to get there. Leave it all in His capable hands—your life, your future, your family, your hopes, your dreams. Everything. Give it to Him.

While we may not know God's will in a given situation, we know He wants us to become more like His beloved Son. Romans 8:29 tells us, "For whom He foreknew, He also predestined to be conformed to the image of His Son." Whatever our purpose in this life, whatever our goals and aspirations, Christ wants us to pour out ourselves so that He may fill us with His Spirit and make us more like Him. More loving, gentle, caring, patient, kind, longsuffering . . . and a host of other positive qualities. They are the fruits of the Spirit, and Christ wants to harvest them in our lives. But only if we're willing. John the Baptist says it succinctly in John 3:30: "He must increase, but I must decrease."

Dear woman of passion, is that your prayer today?

 *A Time for Reflection*

1. How would you describe your times of prayer and Bible study? What is the greatest challenge you face in maintaining a consistent devotional time with God? If you find it nearly impossible to read the Bible regularly, try washing with the Word. Resolve to read at least a chapter before getting out of bed in the morning.

2. Imagine what an ideal mini-retreat with God would be like for you. Where would it be? What time of day? What activities would be most important to you (prayer, Bible reading, meditation, singing, memorizing Scripture, relaxing, listening to God in the silence)? What would it take for you to establish a personal retreat time in your daily schedule?

 *A Time for Action*

1. Write in your journal, describing the sort of mini-retreat you wish to establish for yourself, including

241

time and place. You may use the twelve steps listed in this chapter to guide you in planning your retreat, or you may come up with ideas of your own to tailor this event to your own lifestyle and wishes. (For example, you may choose to have a steaming cup of tea or other refreshment at hand during your mini-retreat. Or you may want to read inspirational literature or devotional books along with your Bible. An occasional walk in the woods or stroll along the beach may add zest and variety to your mini-retreats.) Whatever you decide to do, keep this time special, a private interval in your day to be anticipated, a relaxed, nurturing occasion for you and God to get better acquainted. Guard your retreat times zealously, for once you've established them, you most certainly will be bombarded with every sort of interruption imaginable.

2. Begin your own Word and prayer journal. From your daily Bible reading, select verses that speak to you in a significant way. Write them in your journal. Then list your praises for the day along with your prayer requests and any other details you consider pertinent. This journal will give you an overview of your spiritual growth and help you keep track of your prayers and God's answers.

16
BEGIN YOUR OWN
PASSIONATE JOURNEY

 It's been quite a journey, hasn't it?

God has taught me some vital things during our time together. I trust He has spoken to you too. When we started our passion journey, I mentioned that it was just the two of us, you and me. But really, it has been the three of us, you and me and God. He still has so much to teach us, so much truth to reveal, so much love to shower on us, so much joy.

How blessed we are that God calls us to a relationship of passion, joy, and delight in Him.

The world is just beginning to discover the secrets of joy and happiness the Bible has spoken of all along. In a recent ABC news special with John Stossel, scientists confirmed what most of us Christians already know: Riches and fame do not make people happy. Once our basic needs for food and shelter are met, more money, bigger homes and more possessions do not increase our happiness and may even make us more unhappy.

What makes us happy?

Researchers say happiness comes from strong personal relationships, from doing satisfying work we're good at, and from having a hope for the future and a purpose in life greater than ourselves. The Bible calls this joy.

Joy, of course, is better than happiness; happiness is superficial, dependent on circumstances. But joy comes from God and springs from the depths of our being regardless of our circumstances.

Joy comes when we have someone to love passionately, something to do wholeheartedly, something to hope for, and a grand and glorious purpose that requires a lifetime dedication. We as believers have all that—a Savior who loves us and desires our love in return, who has called us to serve Him and bring souls into His kingdom. And we have the hope and assurance of eternal life in heaven with our Savior. This is the source of joy—loving Him, serving Him, and saving others.

Joy is a frequent theme in Scripture. Numerous verses speak of our joy in the Lord. In Psalm 16:11, David praises the Lord, saying, "You will show me the path of life; in Your presence is fullness of joy; at Your right hand are pleasures forevermore." Psalm 43:4 tells us, "Then I will go to the altar of God, to God my exceeding joy; and on the harp I will praise You, O God, my God." Psalm 32:11 says, "Be glad in the LORD and rejoice, you righteous; and shout for joy, all you upright in heart." Ah, pure joy! For what more can we ask than the joy that comes from basking in our heavenly Father's love?

The Father's love has seen me through all the crises of my life.

As a teenager, when I was tempted to surrender my virginity, it wasn't the church, or a set of commandments, or the warnings of others that kept me pure. It was my

Father's love. I was so in love with Jesus that I didn't want to do anything to hurt or disappoint Him.

When I thought I had cancer, it was the Father's love that gave me strength.

When my baby died, it was the Father's love that comforted me.

When I am anxious about the future, it's the Father's love that reassures me.

As women of passion, we must show the Father's love.

SHARE CHRIST'S PASSION

We've talked at length about passion, but there is one meaning we haven't considered, perhaps the most important definition of all. According to *Webster's New World Dictionary,* the word *passion* means "a suffering, especially that of Christ . . . the agony and sufferings of Jesus during the crucifixion or during the period following the Last Supper."

Can you imagine what Jesus must have felt as He hung on the cross for us? As the awesome totality of humankind's squalid, loathsome sins were heaped on Jesus' broken body, for the first and only time Christ felt what it was like to be separated from His Father. Imagine the pain Jesus must have experienced as God the Father turned His back on Him.

Only a short time before, God had proclaimed, "This is My beloved Son, in whom I am well pleased." But now, as the fetid sins of all the people who had ever lived or were yet to be born were heaped on Christ, God had to turn His face away. A holy God couldn't look upon sin. And Jesus, who knew no sin, had become sin for us. That grim, ghastly moment of spiritual separation was far more devastating to Jesus than anything men could inflict on His body. As He tasted God's appalling silence and rejection, 245

He cried out in torment, "My God, My God, why have You forsaken Me?"

Christ endured the penalty for our sins and the anguish of separation from God for the joy that was set before Him. We are that joy. We are the reason Jesus allowed Himself to experience alienation from His Father God. Because He loved us so much. Loved us more than His own life. For us He conquered death and rose from the grave. He reclaimed His position at the right hand of the Father, where He makes intercession for us and defends us against Satan's attacks.

As women of passion, we need to become passionate about the things that Christ was passionate about. Jesus was a joyful, vigorous, impassioned man. He was passionate about people—children, His mother, His followers, wounded people, hurting people, the hungry, the ill, the grieving. He wept with those who wept. He had a passion to save the lost and be about His Father's business. He was passionate about spending time with His heavenly Father and doing the Father's will.

We, too, need to be passionate about bringing others to faith in Christ, ministering to hurting hearts, helping those who are ill, needy, or grieving. We, too, need to be about our Father's business and doing the Father's will.

And as women of passion, we need to be prepared to teach younger women what it means to love God with all their heart, mind, soul, and strength, and to love others as themselves. We need to instruct, guide, nurture, and encourage young girls to live holy, unblemished lives for God by the power of the Holy Spirit. We need to be examples to them, demonstrating godly love, wisdom, strength, and grace.

In Titus 2:4–5, Paul instructs the older women to "admonish the young women to love their husbands, to love their children, to be discreet, chaste, homemakers, good, obedient to their own husbands, that the word of God may not be blasphemed."

Now, if I didn't know better, I would assume Paul was speaking to women of our own day, for aren't these the same hot-button issues facing twenty-first-century women? With divorce running rampant in our society and children killing children in our schools, we may conclude that many wives and moms need some counsel and direction in properly loving and nurturing their husbands and children. (I'm not letting husbands off the hook; Paul has a lot of pertinent instruction for men too.)

The question is, Where can today's young women go to learn how to establish godly homes and families? Examples of successful marriages are hard to come by these days. Even in our churches, the dysfunctional or nontraditional family has become the norm.

That's why Paul's counsel to older women is so important. Those of us who have already raised our families need to accept the challenge to befriend, encourage, and nurture the younger women in our churches and communities. That doesn't mean we should lord it over them and be critical or judgmental, insisting they do things our way. Rather, we should humbly make ourselves available, walking alongside those who are needy and struggling, upholding them in prayer, cheering them on, and being a loving example in word and deed.

I would encourage you younger women to seek out an older woman in your church or community who might be willing to mentor you. This is especially important if you have no immediate family to offer support— no mom, grandmothers, sisters, or aunts nearby. Some women's ministries set up programs matching older and younger women in discipling relationships. Maybe that's something your church would like to consider.

Many of us fail to realize the significant role we as women play in our churches today. We assume the men

247

are carrying the lion's share of responsibility and that we are minor players. But according to a recent survey by the Barna Research Group, women are the backbone of most church congregations in the United States today. While women represent a hefty 60 percent of the attendees, they are also noted for "their high degree of spiritual depth." Compared to men, women are more likely to participate in adult Sunday school, disciple others, have devotions, read the Bible, share their faith with others, donate to the church, and pray.[1]

Their influence isn't limited to the church. Women are also more likely than men to be the spiritual leaders and role models in their families. So there it is—we as women carry a huge responsibility for the spiritual welfare and growth of our families, our churches, and our communities. In many cases, we are the only ones standing in the gap and providing spiritual sustenance for those in our circle of love.

What an awesome challenge we face, what a clear mandate to salvage those around us who have lost their moorings and slipped into a sea of spiritual chaos. We can rescue them. We can rouse those who have drifted into spiritual sluggishness and malaise. We can make a difference for Christ in our families, churches, and communities.

Don't be afraid. God promises to be with us and help us. "The Lord is near to all who call upon Him, to all who call upon Him sincerely and in truth. He will fulfill the desire of those who reverently and worshipfully fear Him. . . . The Lord takes pleasure in those who reverently and worshipfully fear Him, in those who hope in His mercy and loving-kindness" (Pss. 145:18–19; 147:11 AMPLIFIED).

So discover your passions, dear friend. Share them with others. Delight in your Savior, and feel God's pleasure. Take a leap of faith. Connected tightly to Christ, you can't fail!

As women of passion, we can set ablaze the cold and hardened hearts around us. In the first century a handful of disciples turned the world upside down with their zeal to spread the gospel. What can we do, we who occupy homes and churches in countless communities across our great land? What can we do to turn our world upside down for Christ?

Now at last it is time for us to part company, time for you to continue your own passionate journey alone with God and to become the eager, impassioned person God created you to be.

My friend, permit me to repeat my prayer from the beginning of this book: May our heavenly Father go with you as you press on in your own voyage of discovery into your heart of hearts, into the hearts of your loved ones, and into the heart of God. May you truly love the Lord, your God, with all your heart, mind, soul, and strength, and others as yourself.

And, dear woman of passion, as you delight in the Lord and commit your deepest desires to God for His glory, let your heart echo David's praise to God in Psalm 16:11: "You will show me the path of life; in Your presence is fullness of joy; at Your right hand are pleasures forevermore."

A TIME FOR REFLECTION

1. Read over the journal you have kept since you started this book. What observations can you make? What changes do you notice in your perspective, your attitudes, your habits, your desires? How have you progressed in your spiritual life? How have you grown in your walk with God? How are you different now than when you started your passion journey? How is your family different?
2. How has our journey together benefitted you the most? In what areas do you feel you still need help?

249

 *A Time for Action*

1. Consider where you are in your personal walk with Christ. Do you feel God may want you to mentor someone not as far along in her spiritual journey? Do you have a specific person in mind? If so, ask God to open the door for you to nurture and encourage this woman. If you feel you need someone to mentor you, ask God to bring such a person into your life. Whether you wish to mentor or be mentored, consider taking steps today in your women's group to establish such a program.

2. After rereading the objectives you set for yourself at the beginning of your passion journey, write in your journal, answering these questions: What goals did you accomplish? What hopes are still unrealized? What still needs to be done to make those desires a reality? In what ways do you better understand yourself today? What insights have you gleaned about those in your circle of love? How have you grown in your relationship with Christ?

3. I urge you to continue writing in your journal indefinitely, freely expressing your heart cries, your needs and desires, and your hopes, goals, and dreams. As you articulate these silent missives of the soul, you will better understand the eager, zealous woman God created you to be. I encourage you also to maintain your daily Word and prayer journal and your mini-retreats with Christ, for He alone is your light, your breath, your food and drink, your lifeblood, your all in all.

   Feast on Him, abide in Him, rejoice in Him always. And may His passion always be yours!

Notes

Chapter 6

1. Carole Gift Page, *Misty* (Grand Rapids: Baker, 2000), 52–53.

Chapter 8

1. Quoted in Cecil B. Murphey, *The Encyclopedia of Christian Marriage* (Old Tappan, N.J.: Revell, 1984), 104.

Chapter 16

1. Survey by the Barna Research Group, *American Family Association Journal* 24, no. 8 (September 2000): 10.

Carole Gift Page has published over forty books, both fiction and nonfiction, with a dozen major Christian publishers. An award-winning novelist, Carole has received the C. S. Lewis Honor Book Award and been a finalist several times for the prestigious Gold Medallion Award and the Campus Life Book of the Year Award.

Carole holds a B.S. degree in art education from Bob Jones University, and she taught creative writing at Biola University for several years. She and her husband, Bill, live in Southern California. They have three children (plus one in heaven) and three grandchildren.

Carole is available for speaking engagements, including one-day events and Woman of Passion retreats. Contact her in care of Fleming H. Revell or email her at:

cgiftpag@jps.net